PROTECTION SPELLS

Learn What Witches, Warlocks and Spiritual
Healers Do To Shield and Defend Against
Negative Energy, Entities, and Psychic Attacks

Vibe with Light
Ashley & Beto Salinas

Contents

If you would like to listen to this book for free, while
you read along, please scan below.

"Witchcraft Cheat Sheet"
And to Thank You Here is our Bonus

To show our gratitude, we wanted to share
a quick cheat sheet with highlights that will
help you connect to your witchy side!

To get your bonus go here

https://betosalinas.activehosted.com/f/3

INTRODUCTION

> The first time I called myself a 'witch' was the
> most magickal moment in my life.
> —Margot Adler

As Margot Adler states, considering and identifying as a witch, warlock, spiritual healer, or overall magick worker is one of the most empowering moments in anyone's life. It allows us to be released from the physical turmoils of our day-to-day lives and start to tap into the energetic flows of the Earth and cosmos.

As witches we, Ashley and Beto Salinas, known as Vibe with Light, were able to start holistically viewing phases and experiences in our lives and then empowering ourselves through magick work, to take action. Realizing that we possessed the power, conscious awareness, and ability to manipulate energy to create more positive, harmonious spaces is something that every magick worker is proud to identify with and relate to.

If you have experienced (or are experiencing) symptoms of a psychic attack, just know that you are not alone! Such energies are always at an influx, and some are even directed toward us. These lingering negative energies can show up in various ways, from financial issues, to health issues, relationship issues, mental health issues, constant strings of bad luck, or simply the feeling of a heavy energy looming over us. These are all factors that we face as human beings. However, our duty and responsibility as magick workers is to ensure that we fight these energies through a combination of our powers, knowledge, and a collection of banishing protection spells, which we explore within this book.

Vibe with Light has been where you are, and through experience we have empowered ourselves with magick, knowledge, and experience; we are here to share these sentiments with you to help *you* empower yourself too. In doing so, extend that magick power to others to protect your loved ones and homes from various negative energies and influences, which include banishing energies cast through curses and hexes. All of this shall be unveiled within this book, from all-round protection spells to powerful banishing spells that protect us and deflect such energies (such as intentional curses) back to the perpetrator.

Furthermore, we will be covering protection spells to help ensure that we and our loved ones are able to live in a peaceful, positive, and protected space: one where we can harness magickal energies from various items (such as amulets, crystals, and herbs) or the cosmos' powers (such as via the Sun's and Moon's power) to recharge our energy shields and become stronger, more powerful magick workers. In essence, Vibe with Light has got you covered! From protecting yourself and your loved ones, to recharging your energy shields and even harnessing positive energies to draw upon abundance and prosperity, the benefits of magick are boundless and it all starts here.

Staying in the Know

There's immense magickal strength, power, and higher intuitive powers (guided by and connected spirits) that comes with being a witch, warlock, or spiritual healer. However, it's always important to remember that great power comes with great responsibility.

One of the responsibilities that we (as witches, warlocks, and spiritual healers) need to keep in mind, is that we ensure that we are protected against any energies that may drain our own. This factor comes in the form of *defensive magick* and *protection spells* that help us to keep our energy safe and recharged. Spell casting requires both intention and energy, which we tend to channel from the energy within and around us (Alaska, 2020). Therefore, protecting this energy and ensuring that we are recharging the energy around us is vitally important in order to ensure that we recharge our own energies, so that we not only keep ourselves and our loved ones protected, but we also have enough energy to channel to be able to cast spells correctly.

With this in mind, what we need to understand with defensive magick and protection spells is that they need to be performed correctly, so that we reap the pure benefits of the rituals and spells. If not, we may end up testing our fate and allowing unforeseen energies or parasites (which are energy drainers) into our world. Additionally, this can also trigger us to experience psychic/spiritual attacks, which we have little to no control over. Therefore, while we have the capabilities to exercise our powers, we want to ensure that we're going into these practices with caution and protection against the unknown and unforeseen.

Psychic or spiritual attacks can come in various forms, from having trouble sleeping, to continuously getting ill or sick, to feeling a heavy weighty feeling that's burdening you and stopping you from experiencing a lighter, freer feeling of happiness. Psychic attacks can even hinder you to the point that you may struggle to function optimally, and may even trigger depression. Psychic or spiritual attacks, more often than not, stem from someone having an ill intent toward you, and consciously or subconsciously, wanting to bring harm to you. With this in mind, this energy can target us and result in various symptoms or side effects, as mentioned above.

Now, while we can focus on good energies and light magick, this does not necessarily help us banish evil or negative energies that enter our space. Therefore, defensive magic, protection spells, and properly cleansing our space is vitally important. We need a balance of both light work *and* defensive magick to ensure that we're protected when we work with magick.

Within this book, we aren't only going to be exploring a list of protection spells and defensive magic: we're also going to explore amulets and objects (such as crystals and other minerals) to keep around us to ensure that we're protected and able to banish specific energies. In this book, we are also not only going to focus on protecting ourselves but also our loved ones, in the event that they are suffering from a spiritual attack or simply need additional protection.

When referring to 'protection,' we don't only cover spiritual protection but also physical protection (in terms of health) and emotional protection, so as to ensure that we lead a safe and peaceful life. By practicing protection spells, defensive magick, and carrying protection amulets with us, we can ensure that we (or our loved ones) are in a safe environment, and this can help us to go about our lives in the physical and spiritual world at ease, knowing that we're safe and secure.

Benefits of Protection Spells

> Magic(k) is rooted in this human lineage of collaborating with the Earth and the heavens to create your life.
>
> —Stinson, 2019

Protection spells can be used for anyone, from ourselves to our loved ones. We can perform protection spells or defensive magick to help anyone who may feel vulnerable or in a low-energy state, deeming them more vulnerable and susceptible to ill-intent spells that may have been placed on them. Additionally, protection spells can simply serve as a safeguard, meaning that even if we don't know that we're necessarily going through a psychic attack (or who the attack was from), we can still safeguard ourselves or our loved ones just in case of any attack. As Stinson states, we, as witches, warlocks and spiritual healers have the power and responsibility to manage the spiritual connection between our earthly bodies and the higher self so that we live our lives as stress-free as possible. This can come in the form of protection, a blessing, or removing obstacles that stand in one's way.

With this responsibility in mind, it's our duty to ensure that we create a space so that the 'goals' of our spellwork or rituals are significant and powerful. By combining our intention with our focus and setting the space, we create a *sacred* space whereby we are able to achieve the goal of our spellwork or rituals. We then need to explore the factors that are required in order to create this sacred space; this is to create a space whereby we have a set intention, a place where we have enhanced focus, and a space that signifies the energies that we are trying to draw upon, channel, redirect, or banish.

> Initializing change is your intention, and whatever consequences follow are also your responsibility.
>
> —Arin Murphy-Hiscook,
> author of *The Green Witch*

When performing protection spells, we want to focus a lot of our attention on the intention of the spell. Protection spells can be extremely powerful when the intention is clear and set, and therefore the spells and magick are used for good, not evil. If the spell/ritual requires specific objects, ingredients, or amulets, then there is even more reason to refine the intention of the spell/ritual much more, to reap the most powerful energies of the spell.

Witch (Nadine, 2017)

Protection spellwork and defensive magick can help offer numerous benefits, from clearing or warding off any negative energy around a person, ward off/banish unhealthy influences, help bring more positivity and happiness into one's life, help one embrace their blessings more (of work, health, and life), help one to keep a more positive attitude and mindset towards life, and finally, help block any ill-intent energies that are targeted or sent toward someone. With this in mind, we can already take away that we don't only have to use protection spells to ward off negative energy or be protected from a psychic attack, but we can also use them to help us or our loved ones embrace a more positive life. If you or a loved one is experiencing a low-vibrational period, a protection spell or defensive magick spell can be performed to assist in rebalancing energy levels and start to fully embrace life once again!

> Two key elements for effective magick spells are belief and focus.
> —*Magic Spells Guide for Beginners*, 2020

Whether you know or have a hunch that you or a loved one requires a protection spell, or you simply want to create more spiritual protection over you or a loved one, the key elements for a powerful protection spell stem from the quote above: belief and focus (which includes a refined intention behind the spell). How can we guide and channel energies if we are unsure of our intentions ourselves? Therefore, it's vitally important that before we even consider magick, we clarify our intention prior to the ritual or spell conduction. Honing in on your focus, energy, and effort put into the spell or ritual can enhance the power of the spell, as well as speed up the process of the spell, leaving you with a more powerful spell in a shorter period.

In addition to this, protection spells clear any/all obstacles within this intention or goal; therefore, the factors of attention, wisdom, and empathy need to be taken into account, as the spells we are going to explore are both powerful and efficient. We also want to ensure that the energies we draw upon, channel, and redistribute are accounted for, so that we responsibly manage these energies. This is why spellcasting should primarily be handled by professionals (witches, warlocks, and spiritual healers) or psychics, as we are most aware of the power of such spells, the energies they draw upon, and the energies we channel.

While spellwork and spellcasting can be most effective when handled responsibly, it must be known that spells require a lot of work. From preparing and refining the intention, preparing the ingredients, objects, amulets, and ritual, to channeling the energies and redistributing them, the entire process is taxing and requires an immense amount of work and preparation. The spells that we are going to explore are extremely powerful; however, it's not a simple process of snapping our fingers or simply chanting a mantra. Therefore, we also need to understand that even though these spells are powerful and efficient, it's still not something one can do with little experience or no preparation work in the early stages. This is why, in this chapter, we are stressing the importance of such preparation and understanding the requirements of spellwork, from an intentional and personal space as a channeller, prior to maneuvering through the spellcasting process.

Finally, spellwork and spellcasting requires a deep understanding of the power of the process as well as the power of the spells. We truly have to believe in the powers of the energies we channel, and this mainly comes from our intention—the intention we place in objects/amulets/chants—and a deep understanding of the power of each spell. For example, if we want to place a protection spell on a loved one for health, there's no point in choosing a spell for a loved one's finances or a general protection spell for clearing any obstacles in their path. While such spells can help clear the general negative energies within that person's path, we want to make sure that our rituals and spells are specific and intentional so that they are as powerful and effective as possible. Therefore, while we work through this, we will also explore the specificity of each spell so that we can use the energies we channel in the most efficient and effective way possible.

Naturally (and understandably so), gaining a deeper understanding, believability, and faith in the spells will not only enhance our intention towards the spell and the spell's goal, but also help us to draw and channel energies much better.

Now, with this in mind, the first notable factors that we should consider as preparation prior to physical preparation of protection spellcasting and defensive magick are to: refine our intention, understand the goal of the spell, cleanse the space, recharge our energies, and have a deep understanding and awareness of the spell and the energies we are channeling, as we are responsible for redirecting the path of energies and, ultimately, the outcome of the spell performed.

PREPARATION AND THE SPELLS

Considering all of the above, it's vitally important that we also take care of ourselves and our space, as this form of 'self-care' is also essential for a channeler to perform a good job. Think of it this way: we can't perform productively in an office job if we don't take care of our own personal needs, such as ensuring that we're looking after our body and mind. We need a good amount of rest, exercise, nutrition, hydration, and even socialization in order to mentally and physically perform at our optimal levels.

Sacred Spaces (Nash, 2017)

Similarly, we can compare an office job to what we as witches, warlocks, and spiritual healers do, as this is *our* profession. It requires our time, energy, and skill sets in order to achieve an end goal. Therefore, when we compare our profession to others, we need to ensure that we look after ourselves (mentally, spiritually, and physically) to ensure that we can perform at our best and reap the best results. Naturally, we need to ensure that we take care of our basic needs, such as sufficient rest, hydration, nutrition, and so forth. However, we also need to ensure that we take care of our spiritual needs. This can be done by ensuring that we recharge our energy levels, cleanse our space and ourselves, and protect our energy (Winkler, 2019).

Creating a sacred space for spellcasting and rituals is essential for the efficiency of the spell or ritual process (*Magic Spells Guide for Beginners*, 2020). Creating this sacred space is a mix of both mental, physical, and spiritual cleansing, protection, and preparation factors. A few ways to remain prepared, as well as prepare your space, for spellwork or rituals are as follows:

- *Cleansing yourself*: This can include taking time to quite literally cleanse yourself in a bath of salts or herbs. Cleansing one's self can be done prior to (or after) an intense ritual, or weekly, however often you feel it necessary. Some witches, warlocks and spiritual healers also like to decorate the bath with candles, ornaments, amulets, or crystals, and even add essential oil to the bath water. If you choose to bathe with crystals around the water, try to ensure that your crystals don't come into contact with the water or salt water, as some crystals, such as selenite, lapis lazuli, malachite, and kyanite do not react well when in contact with water.

- *Cleansing the space*: This can be by simply keeping the physical space clean and neat, as a clean space can help us to enhance our focus and channel our energies much more easily. Once the physical space is organized, we can move onto cleansing the air; this can involve lighting candles, incense, bundles of herbs such as sage, and ringing bells, chimes, or banging drums to banish or move any negative or stagnant energies. You can walk around the area while burning incense or herbs, or use your instrument of choice to ensure that the entire area is covered and cleansed. You can also be more intentional with your cleansing ritual by walking in a circle with a bundle of herbs, or reaching each quadrant of the space (the northernmost, southernmost, easternmost, and westernmost points of the area that you are cleansing).

- *Choosing a specific color*: Doing this for your spellcast or ritual can also help to properly carry out the spell. Specific colors are used to signify different intentions and energies; therefore, specifying and placing intention in the colors we wear while spellcasting or performing a ritual can help us to call in and channel energies with much greater ease. A general guide for the colors of clothing are as follows:

  o   White signifies cleansing, understanding, finding clarity, establishing order and spiritual growth.
  o   Black signifies transformation and banishing negative energies.
  o   Red can help signify and strengthen love spells as well as be worn for health rituals.
  o   Orange signifies encouragement and power.

o   Yellow helps enhance communication spells and divination.

o   Green will help with money spells, prosperity, good luck, fertility rituals, and spells for finances or employment.

o   Blue helps with healing rituals, as well as intensifying one's psychic powers.

o   Violet can help with divination and balance.

o   Silver can help with psychic development, meditation and warding off negative energies.

o   Gold can assist with drawing in energies for health, success, divination and good fortune spells.

o   Grey can help with blinding negative influences and assist with clarity on complex decision making.

o   Indigo signifies spiritual healing and meditation.

o   Pink helps to signify love spells and romance, spiritual awakenings, and assist with children's magic.

These colors can differ depending on the type of ritual or culture you're from. Therefore, these colors simply serve as a guide and can assist with the spellcasting or ritual, however the colors you choose can change depending on your own personal circumstances or preferences. The colors you choose can help you to draw in the right energies if you need to perform a specific spell; think of the color choice as offering extra assistance.

•   *Creating a boundary or casting a circle*: This can also help with ritual preparation. Casting a circle or creating a boundary can serve as extra protection to ensure that *only* the spirits, energies, or beings that you're dealing with can enter the circle. This can greatly help to better control which energies you want to draw upon, channel, or banish, as well as which beings are affected by the spell or ritual. One of the more common ways to cast a circle for ritual preparation is to mark their boundary area with blessed water, oils, or salt. Other forms of casting a circle are to mark the edges of the circle with an athame (a ceremonial blade, generally with a black handle) dipped in saltwater or to create a boundary with meditation, by creating a protective bubble of energy around the space. Either way, casting a circle or creating a boundary for the space is another form of protection (as is cleansing one's self and the space) to ensure that the spell or ritual is as efficient and powerful as possible.

- *Emphasizing the light*: This can be done by lighting a candle or multiple candles to set the ambiance of the space. Candles can also help us to focus in and channel energies: the more powerful the flame, the stronger the connection to the spiritual realm or the stronger the connection with spirit. These candles can be different from the candles that you are going to be using in your ritual; they simply serve as ambiance and to assist with focusing. You can also choose the color of the candles to help signify the energies you'd like to invite in (in accordance with the colors described above).

The above points are merely a few of the most common forms of preparing for a spell or ritual. You can choose which points you'd like to use in order to prepare; however, if you are performing rituals that are taxing, it may benefit you to ensure that all the above points are checked off.

In addition to the above points, there are a few other preparation techniques that some witches, warlocks, and spiritual healers do, just to ensure that the environment and atmosphere is as protected and controlled as possible for the ritual or spellwork. One of those methods is to cover all clock faces within the space you're practicing; this is to ensure that the space in which you're performing the ritual is perceived as being held in a 'timeless' state. This can also be enhanced by drawing all of the curtains and closing or locking all of the windows and doors in order to avoid interruptions. Drawing all of the curtains can also help enhance the feel that the ritual is being performed in a timeless state.

Finally, many witches, warlocks, and spiritual healers tend to practice protecting their mental health and state throughout the day by actively practicing meditation, grounding themselves by listening to meditative music or prayers, especially on the day of an intense ritual. Ensuring that you check off a few or all of these preparation techniques prior to a ritual or spellcasting will greatly help you to feel properly prepared and in control of the ritual. It's also important to note that the above pointers cover cleansing one's self, cleansing the space, surrounding ourselves with symbolic colors that will help us to draw in and channel the right energies, *and* ensuring that we create a space that we can control and channel energies. All of these factors are the key preparation factors for a responsible witch, warlock, or spiritual healer. If we deem ourselves professional in our field, and want to reap the most benefits from our practices, then we need to ensure that we're checking off the above-mentioned factors, as this is our responsibility, just as much as we are responsible for the outcome of the spells or rituals conducted.

Defense Against Attacks

Psychic attacks (also known as spiritual attacks) cover a broad spectrum of topics that come in the form of low-vibrational energies. These low-vibrational energies can latch onto someone or be directly sent from someone with ill-intent (such as a target or curse).

Psychic attacks can essentially be described as someone's aura being compromised by negative (low-vibrational) energy. This low-vibrational energy can show itself in various forms, such as physical or mental health issues, financial issues, a constant string of unforeseen bad luck, an overall sense that there is something dark looming over you, a constant string of anxiety or panic attacks, a constant state of feeling an impending doom, and so forth. Psychic attacks can come in the form of anything inexplicable that may come across as bad luck or simply anything in our lives that forces us to stay in a low-vibrational state. It can leave us in a state of depression, stress, nausea, anxiety, to name a few emotions, and can trigger our emotional state so much that we may even end up falling more sick or experiencing even more bad luck due to our energy shield being low and vulnerable from an attack.

Within this book, we are going to explore ways to directly protect ourselves and loved ones from such low-vibrational states, and therefore ensure that our energy shield is strong enough to withstand such attacks.

Whether the attack comes in the form of depression, anxiety, bad health issues, or other situations, such as relationship or financial problems, we are going to cover specific protection spells to banish such energies from our paths, remove obstacles, and bless ourselves and our path (or our loved ones and their paths). However, before we explore ways to protect ourselves from such attacks, we need to understand the *types* of attacks and their 'symptoms' per sé, so that we can identify them and then choose spells, rituals, and amulets accordingly.

The spells that we are going to explore will be specific to the symptoms that we face or the factors in our lives that may be triggered by the attack (for example, having relationship issues or health issues). As we have come to understand, spellwork and rituals are much more powerful when the intention is refined, and when we add on essential items with intentions placed in them as well (for instance, wearing white with the intention of cleaning and finding clarity). When we combine the clarity of these intentions along with a greater understanding of the type of attack we're dealing with, we can then have a better understanding of the type of spell or ritual needed. Similarly, we can also use the knowledge of a type of attack to help us choose ways to prepare for a spell or ritual (such as wearing specific colors, using specific crystals, lighting specific candles, burning specific herbs, and so forth).

The combination of understanding the intention behind the preparation for a spell or ritual (which we explored in the previous chapter), the type of attack we're dealing with (and its intention), and the spell or ritual we're performing, can all help equate to an extremely powerful, specific, intentional, and efficient ritual or spell.

When we have a clear understanding of the intentions behind our preparations, the intention behind and the knowledge of the type of attack, as well as the ritual or spell that we're performing or casting, we can also ensure that reaching the goal of the ritual or spell isn't only effective, it's also resourceful in the sense that we don't need to exhaust too much unnecessary time and energy into the spell. While we want to ensure that we protect and recharge our energy shield, we want to responsibly handle the spells and rituals so that we don't burn out from the work we do.

Think about it this way: if we budget to fill up our tank with gas at the beginning of every week, we want to try and avoid any unnecessary or unforeseen detours throughout the week that may use up the gas. We want that fuel to last the entire week in order to ensure that we travel to our destinations without hesitating about how much fuel is left or needing to refill the tank. Similarly, we want to fill up our energy shield and manage it responsibly so that we don't feel exhausted halfway through a ritual. Therefore, we want to be as efficient and responsible as possible to ensure that we are prepared for what energies and forces we will need to deal with. This is especially a notable factor for witches, warlocks, and spiritual healers because protecting our energy is part of running a responsible practice, and part of this responsibility is to ensure that we don't exhaust our energies in an irresponsible or ignorant manner.

With this in mind, understanding the different types of attacks one can experience can also help us prepare for how much energy we need to draw in, channel, and exhaust in order to face and banish negative forces in our (or our loved ones') space. When we gain a better understanding of such attacks, we can also better prepare ourselves for such rituals or spellwork to protect us and clear the space. Naturally, with time, this understanding of different types of attacks combined with lived experience of dealing with such attacks can help us to become wiser, more experienced, and more powerful as a witch, warlock, or spiritual healer, and in turn, this will make the processes or such rituals or spells much more efficient and powerful.

Types of Attacks

To quickly refer back to our metaphor of filling a car's tank with fuel, the 'destinations' where the car will travel to and from throughout the week can easily be compared to the goals that are the outcome of our rituals and spellwork. The type of ritual or spellwork can be compared to the route we choose to travel to our destination (goal), and the type of attack can be compared to the type of road we travel and the obstacles that we may face on the journey to our destination.

We can compare the types of attacks we face to the type of road our car travels on, because the type of attack will determine which obstacles or problems we may face when travelling to our destination. This type of road (attack) will also determine how much energy (fuel) we will need and how much preparation (type of vehicle or transport) we will need to reach that destination. With this understanding, we can essentially say that gaining knowledge of the type of attacks one may face can help us better prepare for the road and get to the destination as quickly, efficiently, and resourcefully as possible.

Now, there are three main kinds of psychic attacks and another two forms of thoughtforms, which can also affect one (the victim) in a similar attack form, essentially leaving us with five main forms of attacks. The attacks are broken up into the categories of the psychic influencer, the psychic vampire, and the attacking witch or warlock. The thoughtforms are broken into intentional thoughtforms and unintentional thoughtforms (Hart, n.d.).

Psychic Influencer

The first type of an attack one can experience is categorized as the *psychic influencer*. This type of attack occurs when an 'influencer' wants to achieve something extremely badly and manifests the bad effects of that desire through the victim of the attack. Generally speaking, the psychic attack is an intentional act as the influencer intentionally wants to desperately achieve something; however in most cases, the influencer is also unaware of the fact that they may be causing or triggering the effects of their desires on the victim. The psychic attack is usually described as somewhat of a selfish act on behalf of the influencer, as they don't necessarily take into consideration the effects of their manifestation of desires upon the victim of the attack.

Psychic attacks can therefore essentially be defined as an extremely subtle form of mind control, whereby the influencer (the one with a desire or goal) will manifest their goal through the victim, and leave the victim's thoughts and emotions influenced by the influencer. A few prime examples of a psychic attack are when the influencer wants you to love them or the influencer wants you to act or think a certain way in order for them to get what they want, such as influencing you to leave a job position so that they can take it, or leaving your romantic partner so that they can pursue that partner. Psychic influencers are generally tied to their victim (of the attack) when they want something that the victim haa or they want to pursue. These attacks generally tend to influence the victim's thoughts, emotions, and actions in order to suit the goal or desire of the influencer.

So, how can we tell who is an influencer? Generally speaking, those responsible for psychic influencer attacks are usually considerably insecure people who unintentionally or unknowingly seek happiness at the expense of others. Influencers usually struggle to create or find happiness within their own life, and are insecure of aspects within their own life, which then transpires into them wanting to (in a sense) steal another's happiness. Now, what's important to understand is that influencers who cause such psychic attacks on others aren't always necessarily deemed as negative or evil influences, as often they are even unaware of the repercussions of their manifestations (through the psychic attack and influence on others). They're simply sitting in a low-vibrational space of insecurity or jealousy, without intentionally or consciously recognizing the repercussions of their actions, thoughts, and motives. However, we must also acknowledge that there are also those influencers who do have ill-intentions and are aware of the repercussions; therefore, we need to be on guard and aware of those individuals.

Now, to move onto how one would know that they're experiencing a psychic influencer attack: one of the main factors to look out for is if we (the victim of the attack) are acting out of accordance with our character, morals, ethics, and beliefs. If you or someone you are assisting is experiencing a sudden change in character, there may be a psychic influencer attack at play. A psychic influencer attack may also affect one's sleep cycle and quality of sleep, and leave the victim suffering from disrupted sleep, nightmares, or even dreams of the influencer who is inflicting the attack.

One way to clarify whether the attack is from a psychic influencer or a spirit is to consider the following: if you're having recurring dreams of someone, then it could be your influencer, and it can stem from a psychic influence attack. Another factor to consider is if you can have a conversation with the 'voice' in your head that is influencing your thoughts, emotions, and actions, then it is probably a spirit. If you aren't able to have a conversation with the voice that is influencing your thoughts, actions and emotions, then it can be a psychic influencer attack.

If you (the victim) are experiencing sudden personality changes that align with someone that you know, then that could stem from a psychic influencer attack, and the influencer could be the person that your sudden personality changes are aligning with. Finally, if you (the victim) are starting to experience memories that aren't your own, it could be a spirit rather than a human influencer. A psychic influencer attack can often be confused with possession, as some of the effects of a psychic influencer attack can resemble similar effects from a possession, such as the sudden change in personality and character.

Therefore, it's important that we explore these questions and factors in order to define whether the attack is coming from a spirit or entity, or from another human being (influencer). Luckily though, whether the attack is from a spirit, entity, or being, one can still cleanse and protect one's self in a similar manner. Therefore, we (as witches, warlocks, and spiritual healers) can treat this attack with protection spells in a symptom-based manner, if we can't seem to pinpoint the exact root of the attack. Additionally, we can also cleanse the victim's space and provide them with protection in the form of banishing spells, protection amulets, and other protection rituals and items (which we will more specifically explore in Chapters 8 through 10).

Psychic Vampire

The second type of attack one may experience is the *psychic vampire*. This form of attack is extremely common and somewhat self-explanatory, as a psychic vampire is essentially defined as a person who drains energy from others with whom they come in contact. These forms of a psychic attack are usually due to the psychic vampire's energy being depleted faster than it can be replenished. Generally speaking, psychic vampires experience a faster depletion of energy because they may have experienced extreme trauma, which they haven't healed from or haven't properly handled; therefore, a psychic vampire will need to (usually unintentionally) feed off of others' energy in order to replenish their own energy levels.

It's extremely common for many people to face, deal, or live with an energy vampire in their lives, and there are many different ways to handle such relationships. However, it is important to note that energy vampires can leave the victim suffering from various side effects due to the victim's energy being drained. A few side effects of a psychic vampire attack include feeling exhausted, depressed, ill, having low-immunity, or simply feeling as though you're in a low-vibrational state. You may feel as though you're struggling to feel happy, excited, motivated, or hopeful due to your energy being drained and this can trigger mental health issues, issues in relationships, issues with productivity in work, or even an overall lower quality of life.

One way to quickly identify if you're dealing with a psychic vampire is if you simply dread interacting with that person. You may also feel as though that person (a psychic vampire) can trigger specific negative emotions in you: for example, you feel anxious, stressed, tired, or sad during or after an interaction with this person. Some psychic vampires are so draining that long-term interaction with them may even leave one feeling depressed or ill after a while.

The first step towards dealing with a psychic vampire is to first identify who that person is, and then try to limit your exposure with them (if possible) and set boundaries so that you can ensure that you don't allow your own energy to be completely drained in the process of overexposed inter-action with them. Second, try to find ways to protect your own energy and replenish your own source of energy in your own time, which can better help you to interact with the psychic vampire without needing to feel sick, drained, depressed, or exhausted. Finally, you can cleanse your space and yourself to remove any negative, weighty energy, and also cast a protective spell or perform a protection ritual in order to ward off the psychic vampire's ability to drain one's energy. Additionally, if the psychic vampire is someone who is approachable and you've managed to catch them in a good mood, you (the victim of the psychic attack) can try to open up a conversation about how their ways can drain energy and offer ways to help ground a psychic vampire so that they can stabilize their own levels of energy without needing to draw energy from others. If this conversation is not an option for the victim and the psychic vampire, then cleansing and protection spells can be the most effective, in this case to ensure that the victim's energy sources are protected and kept at sustainable levels.

Psychic Vampire (Kalhh, 2016)

Attacking Witch

The third type of an attack is the *attacking witch*. This type of attack is definitely an intentional one that is directly sent from a witch or warlock with malicious intent. These forms of psychic attacks can be extremely dangerous or tricky to deal with and difficult to shake off, as these forms of attacks are done by directly casting a spell on you (the victim).

The attacking witch doesn't always necessarily relate to a bad or evil spell that needs to be cast; there are spells cast for other intentions (such as a love spell) that can be directed at you (the victim). However, the spell can sometimes manifest in absurd manners and show up in signs, such as strings of unforeseen bad luck, weird accidents, or experiencing unusual occurrences that can block you from achieving something that doesn't align with the intentions of the spell cast on you. For example, if a love spell is cast on you, it may inhibit you from pursuing love that isn't in alignment with the love spell that was cast. You may experience weird blocks or unusual occurrences, which constantly stop you from freely pursuing love, if those interests don't align with the spell cast on you.

Similarly, an attacking witch can also cast a spell for work, health, relationships, and various other reasons with a specific intention in mind of the attacking witch; these spells aren't cast without intention. In most cases, the attacking witch spell won't directly, physically harm you, but it can show itself in weird and absurd manners, such as experiencing a string of random unfortunate events that inhibit you from achieving something.

The biggest issue with the attacking witch spell is that it is extremely hard to identify at first, as it simply seems like a string of absurd events, or simply brushed off as a period of bad luck. However, you can identify an event of an attacking witch psychic attack if you're experiencing a string of unusual bad luck or unusual accidents, experiencing weird thoughts and feelings that don't align with your true character, if you feel as though you're suddenly cursed, if you notice a specific pattern of events that constantly inhibit or block you from achieving or experiencing something, and various other unusual or absurd patterns. Another way to tell whether you're suffering an attack from the psychic is if you or the victim have strings of nightmares (accompanying a string of bad luck), which can oftentimes involve dreams of a magician or witch.

Experiencing an attack from the attacking witch can also sometimes be confused with an attack from the psychic influencer; however, witches, warlocks, and spiritual healers will usually be able to tell the difference between an attacking witch or a psychic influencer as their intuition can pick up on the intention of the spell cast on the victim. Witches, warlocks, and spiritual healers can also tell the difference between an attacking witch and a psychic influencer by knowing when magick is being intentionally used (which is the case with an attacking witch), whereas a psychic influencer is generally unintentional and hardly ever involves magick. Some witches (who cast an attacking witch spell) tend to also let the person know if they've cast a spell on them, as this usually comes as an ego boost for them and they will want you to know that they are the ones in power and have cast the spell.

Attacking witch spells can be cleared through cleansing baths, rituals, and spells (as explored in Chapter 4). If the spell continues to persist, one may seek a witch's help to cast a protection spell or ritual to ward off the energy and may even perform a banishing spell for further protection, in the event that the attacking witch may want to recast a spell onto the victim.

Attacking Witch. (Justino, 2016)

Thoughtforms

Moving onto thoughtforms: these are psychic attacks that are created through human thought, be it intentional or unintentional. Thoughtforms are also known as 'tulpa' or 'egregore,' and are a culmination 0f will, intention, and emotion. When thoughtforms are created, they become their own beings (in spirit form) and separate from their original maker. Thoughtforms can begin to act independently, away from the original maker or not. Thoughtforms can also function in numerous ways, just as much as the original maker can imagine the thoughtform to be and function.

Thoughtforms, in this sense, can seem quite scary as the possibilities of using one's mind to create a thoughtform are infinite. However, most thoughtforms are usually quite peaceful in the initial stages. Peaceful and sentient thoughtforms are created in the event that the intentions are pure, which is generally the case. However, it is important to acknowledge that there are ill-intended people out there who can also create thoughtforms to be evil, and this is where things start to get a little tricky for the victims of such thoughtforms.

As previously stated, thoughtforms are broken up into two categories: *intentional thoughtforms* and *unintentional thoughtforms*. Intentional thoughtforms are spirits created by magick workers (such as you and me), and are usually created for specific purposes; therefore, they are created with good, clear, and pure intentions. Intentional thoughtforms can be created for a number of reasons. A magick worker may create a thoughtform to help them gather more information to help them with spellwork or research, or help keep watch of the magick worker's space of work or home (so as to guard the space). Although these intentions are pure and positive, we cannot ignore the fact that there are some intentional thoughtforms that are created through negative intent. Such (ill-intended) intentional thoughtforms have the ability to follow others, harass them, and even try to harm others by causing accidents. Such ill-intended intentional thoughtforms are usually created (by magick workers) with specific malicious intention on a specific person or group of people, whom the intentional thoughtform will target and follow.

It's important to note, however, that even though thought-forms are generated by creators, thoughtforms are still spirits. Thoughtforms are independent beings, even though they were created. Therefore, thoughtforms should still be treated as we would treat any other spirit, regardless of where they were created, as spirits still require basic respect in order for us to be able to communicate and interact with them.

Intentional thoughtforms are generally quite difficult to identify for people who aren't sensitive to spirits and energies. However, for those of us who are sensitive to energies and spirits, regular exposure to such entities can help us to better exercise our ability to not only identify a thoughtform, but also identify the creator of the thoughtform (its origin). Divination methods can also be used to help identify the origin of the thoughtform.

When a thoughtform is identified (and you find that it is latching onto you or following you), you should first attempt to banish it, regardless of whether the thoughtform is peaceful or not. Thereafter, cleanse the space and yourself, ward off the spirit, and bind the magick worker who is responsible for the creation of the thoughtform. If the thoughtform is still new or less developed and you're a more experienced magick worker, you can temporarily try to bind the thoughtform and use it to receive more information on its origin and even intention. However, if the thoughtform is more independent and developed, it may have developed the ability to lie, become secretive, and may even be able to protect its owner in the process.

The second type of a thoughtform is an unintentional thoughtform. Unintentional thoughtforms are usually created by psychic influencers, but those who have become excessive or obsessive with their intentions. When a psychic influencer starts to desperately desire something or obsess over something (or someone), the influencer has the potential to unintentionally create an entire entity: a thoughtform. Unintentional thoughtforms hold the characteristics of being considerably erratic and unpredictable with their behavior. These characteristics are generally due to the fact that the creator of the thoughtform was not aware that they had accidentally created a thoughtform; therefore, the intentions of the thoughtform are unclear, and the thoughtform was created primarily from excessive and erratic emotions from the psychic influencer.

In addition to the above characteristics, the thoughtform may also have violent and angry tendencies. This is generally due to the fact that the thoughtform is poorly cared for because the creator (the psychic influencer) is unaware of the thoughtform's existence, and will therefore not look after the thoughtform. Due to the fact that the thoughtform was also created accidentally and from the deepest emotions (obsession and desperation) of the psychic influencer, the thoughtform will start to take on and encompass those deep desires of the creator. The thoughtform may also become quite persistent in attempting to manifest those desires of the psychic influencer, as it is all that the thoughtform knows: those desires/obsessions and the emotions of the psychic influencer.

With this in mind, unintentional thoughtforms can be a bit difficult to manage as they're extremely unpredictable and volatile. As we have also come to understand, we need to treat all thoughtforms with the same respect and patience as we would with any other spirit, as thoughtforms (be it intentional or unintentional) do think and feel independently. Therefore, the best way to manage such spirits is to break the bond that the thoughtform has to its owner, as this will at least help the thoughtform to remove itself from a creator/owner who is not caring for it. Unfortunately, we cannot rehabilitate thoughtforms in the way one can rehabilitate a hurting spirit, which is why the next kindest gesture to help manage a thoughtform is to first detach it from its owner.

Now, detaching the thoughtform from its owner only solves half of the problem, as the thoughtform will still be holding the same thoughts, feelings, and characteristics as before: it will still hold the same obsessive and erratic characteristics from which it was created. Therefore, after detaching the thoughtform from its owner, one will need to cleanse one's self (the target of the thoughtform), as well as bind the psychic influencer who created the thoughtform. Thereafter, one will need to ward one's self to break off any energetic ties and indirect effects that were attached to the psychic influencer. Finally, the thoughtform will need to be dismantled, banished, or bound; this is up to the preference and power of the magick worker who is performing the protection rituals.

While we can identify and protect ourselves in the spiritual realm, it's also important to be aware of the physical characteristics and capabilities of humans on the physical plane. For example, those who are psychic influencers can come in the form of stalkers, a toxic "ex," or someone who is dangerously obsessed with you or sees you as competition, which could even be a business partner, a business competitor, or a jealous spouse. Psychic vampires can also signal physically dangerous people, such as those who are narcissistic or tend to gaslight others, leaving the victim of a psychic vampire feeling stuck in an abusive relationship with the psychic vampire. Therefore, while we can (and are) going to explore ways to cleanse and protect ourselves and our space, we still need to be aware of the physical world's dangers and where the potential threats could be. Sometimes, we can even use such energetic threats as a way to identify the root cause (person and their intentions) to then determine how to better protect ourselves in the physical realm.

Why Do We Need Protection?

Simply judging from the above set of psychic attacks, we can understandably see that psychic attacks can leave us feeling exhausted and drained in all senses of the word. Psychic attacks can also happen to anyone and everyone, especially because psychic attacks can come in the form of so many different interactions, whether we're interacting with someone and feeling drained, stuck in an abusive relationship, receiving envious looks from a jealous work colleague, or even being directly targeted by a maliciously intended magick worker; there are many spaces where we are vulnerable to such attacks. What's more concerning is that as magick workers ourselves, we are even more exposed and susceptible to such energies and attacks, because we handle so many energies on a daily basis. Therefore, protection is vitally important for us to continue with our work, without putting ourselves at risk of a psychic attack because we were ignorant, lazy, or ill-prepared!

We, as magick workers, are also much more aware of negative energies and harmful spells than others who would often brush such events and instances off as mere 'bad luck.' Therefore, this factor should also highlight the importance of proper and regular protection and cleansing, because we see how much negative energy and spellwork exists. We also expose ourselves to all sorts of energies, spells, curses, and various other situations; therefore, we need additional protection for the amount of energies and situations to which we are exposed.

Professional magick workers (such as you and me) need to ensure that we exercise this responsibility of ours to provide proper protection to ourselves and others, so that we also become stronger, more experienced magick workers. The more we routinely practice protection spells and rituals, the stronger and more powerful we become, and thus, the more powerful the protection spells and rituals are. In this book, we explore ways to protect ourselves and our loved ones from psychic attacks and the side effects that an attack may trigger, whether it be emotional or mental triggers, such as depression and anxiety, or physical triggers, such as strings of bad luck or illnesses. However, with this in mind, we must reiterate that while these protection spells will help us and our loved ones free ourselves from the clutches of evil energies, spirits, and curses, we still need to remember that there are many physical world dangers to account for, such as ill-intended or malicious people.

Therefore, while it's important that we practice protection spells and rituals, we still need to maneuver through life with caution and care, in the event that someone who has directed a psychic attack on the victim does actually have the capability to be physically dangerous. Dealing with such people will require additional physical protection, as well as protection spells and rituals. However, it's important to note that such protection spells and rituals can still hold value to keep the victim protected as much as possible. For example, if a victim of a psychic attack was in an abusive relationship with a psychic vampire, a protection spell can help to further protect the victim by recharging their energy levels, enhancing their intuitive senses to be able to handle the situation in the safest way possible, increasing spiritual protection over the victim, reducing the victim's side effects of the psychic attack (such as stress, anxiety, and depression), and even helping the victim gain the strength to take charge of the situation and stand their ground.

The victim of an attack will need to apply their own thinking to the situation in order to determine whether additional physical protection is needed in order to handle their situation and attack. For example, if the psychic vampire is abusive or dangerous, the victim may want to reach out to law enforcement to provide additional security and protection when handling the matter. This is merely one example of how protection spells and rituals can help with our day-to-day situations.

Protection spells and rituals are also not *only* for times of attacks, such as the above example. Protection spells and rituals can also keep our energies guarded and shielded so that we don't place ourselves in vulnerable spaces and get tangled in such situations. Protection spells can also provide us with the strength to be able to see ourselves through tough situations (or attacks), which are inevitable. For example, if a negative experience was in our cards or part of our fate, then we at the very least have ourselves protected spiritually and energetically enough to handle that experience.

Finally, we can also explore the prime example of how there has been an increase in the greater interest for mindfulness and meditation within the general public. This spark in interest suggests that many people are starting to realize the importance of taking time out to protect their space and their energy. Many people are starting to prioritize taking care of themselves in order to ensure that their energy levels are guarded, and that they aren't hitting burnout or feeling exhausted. With this factor in mind, the importance of protecting our energy is becoming more and more a priority, and even more prevalent is that protection spells for our energy is for anyone and everyone. Every single one of us is susceptible to having our energy drained or having negative energies or curses, which can target and follow us. Therefore, to put it simply, protection is abundant and always a good idea to consider maintaining.

In addition to the importance of protecting ourselves, our space, and our energy, protection spells and rituals also play a vitally important role in bringing energies in the world back into balance. Sometimes there can be spaces that are extremely weighty or negative spaces, and these spaces can start to feel chaotic and even dangerous. Magick workers can make use of protection spells and rituals to bring about much needed balance, to ensure that the space is cleansed, safe, and falling back into a healthy, balanced cycle flow of energy.

How Much Protection Is Enough?

There are a variety of protection spells that we are going to explore throughout this book, all of which are dependent on the severity of the symptoms of the curse placed or the state of the victim of the negative energies.

As we have discussed above, and referring back to the car and destination metaphor, we want to ensure that we have enough fuel (energy) to ensure that we arrive at our destination. Understanding what type of road (psychic attack) can help us to understand how much energy we need to see the journey through. Protection spells can greatly help us ensure that our energy levels are managed sustainably, and ensure that it is protected from being drained unnecessarily. With this in mind, we can then determine how much protection is required for us to keep our energy levels sufficiently guarded.

There are four key types of protection spells that we can compare to the type of attack or situation we are dealing with: strong protection spells, protection chants, protection spells for someone else, and protection spells against negative people (*Protection Spells*, 2021).

The first type of protection spell is a *strong protection spell*. Strong protection spells are mainly used on someone when they are not immediately near us and are about to enter a dangerous space, regardless of whether they are aware of it or not. Strong protection spells can work perfectly and powerfully for those who are far away from us and urgently need additional spiritual protection. Strong protection spells are also quick to perform, require only a few steps, and can be extremely powerful and effective when performed with a strong and clear intention.

The second type of a protection spell is a *protection spell chant*. Chants are powerful ways to help increase the power and enhance your focus within your spellwork or ritual. Chants also serve as a powerful form of a meditation to help the magick worker (and others partaking in the spell or ritual) to shift from a conscious state of mind toward a subconscious state of mind, thus assisting in enhancing and refining our subconscious focus on the intention of the spell or ritual. Protection spell chants can be chanted in a simple mantra format or accompanied by drums or other musical instruments to draw in the energy.

Protection spell chants are extremely powerful and unique in the sense that the chants can provide a gorgeous and easy musical way to help us easily remember the chant (or easily join in on a chant). Protection spell chants can also help the chanters to draw in more emotion and power into the chant, making the chant more powerful and effective. Chants have also become extremely popular in the modern day, but present themselves in the form of positive affirmations. Many people start their day with positive affirmations in order to protect their energy and health, as well as recharge their energies for the day. Positive affirmations are a prime example of the subconscious effect that chanting has in our lives. It leaves us feeling more powerful, confident, protected, and intentional when maneuvering through life.

The third type of a protection spell is a *protection spell for someone else*; this protection spell can be used hand-in-hand with the strong protection spell or not. A protection spell for someone else is usually used when the person is physically far away from you and you want to offer them some additional protection. Protection spells for others can be used for additional protection, or it can also be used (in addition to a strong protection spell) for others when you feel that the person may be entering a dangerous or bad situation.

The last type of protection is a *protection spell against negative people*: this can greatly help those who are dealing with psychic vampire attacks or even psychic influencers. The world is filled with both good and bad people, and we interact with numerous people on a daily basis who all have different intentions and energies. Coming into contact or interacting with negative people can leave one stuck in a toxic situation, leaving the victim feeling drained, in a low-vibrational state, or even worse, harmed or placed in physically dangerous situations. Using protection spells can help one to continue going about their lives without risking their space and energy tainted by coming into contact with a negative person.

One form of a protection spell against negative people is to put together a bottle spell, which we will be exploring within Chapter 5: Protection Objects and Idols. Bottle spells are a potent form of a protection spell, especially when the intention placed on it is clear and powerful. The more powerful and experienced the magick worker, the more powerful and potent the protection bottle. Protection bottles can be carried around for our own protection or given to a loved one to protect them. Protection spell bottles can also cross over as a form of a powerful protection spell, as it can provide protection for those who are far away from us and entering a dangerous space or situation.

With the above factors in mind, we need to use our discretion on how much protection is sufficient for the type of situation with which we're dealing. Naturally, the more we practice protection spellwork and rituals, the more powerful our magick becomes, and thus, the fewer spells or rituals we will need for each situation, as we are able to channel more energy and magick into fewer, more specific spells and rituals.

However, as a beginner witch, warlock, or spiritual healer, one will need to gain a deep understanding of the situation (type of attack) they are dealing with and be able to decipher how much negative energy is surrounding the situation. From there on, we can aim to gain more detail on the characteristics of that negative energy. For example: Is it targeting only health-related issues? Is it creating blocks in someone's love life? Is it only lingering in a specific space or is it following the person throughout the day? These factors can help us refine direct and specific protection spells to counteract those negative energies, thus making the protection spellwork much more powerful and intentional. If there is simply a negative energy lingering around, then one may want to simply cleanse the space. If there isn't any sign of negative energy but you would just like to offer someone any additional protection in the event that they encounter something negative, then blessing an object, amulet, or creating a protection spell bottle can be viable options.

Finally, as a magick worker, our *intuition* is one of the most accurate and sensitive of senses to trust. We should always aim to factor in our intuition; even if we can't detect any negative energies currently, our sixth sense will always be able to give us a head's up. Therefore, if your intuition is telling you to provide protection for yourself or someone you know, try to follow that sign rather than wait for more proof that there is a negative energy lingering. It's better to catch these sorts of things early on, as it's easier to cleanse, ward off, and banish such energies before they manage to get a stronger hold on us!

With this in mind, we refer back to the question: How much protection is enough protection? And to simply put it, the answer depends on a few factors: our understanding of the situation; our discrepancy on the power, strength, or attachment of the negative energy present; the amount of power and experience we (as magick workers) possess; and finally, ensuring that we (the magick workers) are also protected enough to protect others. We need to ensure that we aren't only protecting others from negative energies, if we're leaving ourselves with a low energy shield and vulnerable to the negative energies we need to face and banish.

Therefore, we should always aim to ensure that we're taking proper care in cleansing and protecting ourselves and our space *first*, before offering our abilities to others to extend spiritual and energetic protection. So, to put it simply: we should generally aim to double our efforts in providing protection, as we need to ensure that we are protected as well, then further provide protection to the person or situation in need.

The Importance of Daily Practices: The Routine of a Magick Worker

s we have come to understand in the previous two chapters, it's our responsibility as magick workers to ensure that we constantly have ourselves and our space cleansed and protected. This is primarily due to the fact that we are constantly exposing ourselves to all sorts of energies, situations, people, spirits, and magick. With this constant exposure, we can be left feeling drained or vulnerable to the energies we deal with if we don't ensure that we take proper care of *our* energy and *our* space.

As we have also come to understand in the previous chapter, we cannot help others if we aren't looking after our own energetic shield and space. We need to ensure that we're energetically equipped, recharged, and protected to ensure that we are able to safely handle energies, and have the strength to restore energetic balance.

With this in mind, it must be a duty of magick workers to create a specific, disciplined daily routine to ensure that we are taking care of our energetic needs. It's always better to ensure that our energy shields are always charged and that we are protected, rather than waiting for something to happen to us. Responsible magick workers will ensure that they are always protected and energetically strong, so that they can go about their day-to-day work properly prepared.

This chapter aims to cover that crucial first step of proper protection in the form of creating a disciplined daily routine. We can similarly compare this chapter to an emergency plane landing: you always need to ensure that you protect yourself first by placing an oxygen mask over your own mouth before moving on to help others. Similarly, we need to ensure that we take care of our own spiritual and energetic needs before working towards assisting others.

Creating a daily or regular spiritual routine is our (as magick workers) way of ensuring that we have our 'oxygen mask' on before helping others. Now, creating and maintaining a spiritual routine may be a difficult task to undertake, as many are unsure of where to even start. Factors, such as the specifications for creating a daily ritual—as well as being disciplined about when to perform the daily ritual, and the powerful energy that a daily ritual offers—are all aspects that can leave a beginner magick worker feeling uncertain of where to even begin. However, as we become more experienced in magick and spellwork, we will be able to refine our daily spiritual routine much more and create a more specific routine that suits our spiritual needs, as we understand those needs much more.

With this in mind, we all have to start somewhere; and within this chapter, we're going to explore that very valuable starting point. Fortunately for us, a daily spiritual routine doesn't need to be extremely elaborate or intricate. It can include a few simple processes each day that ensure that you and your space are constantly cleansed and protected. If there are any lingering negative energies or attacks, they can be managed with much more ease this way, as a cleansed and protected space makes it much harder for negative energies or malicious spirits to linger around for longer than intended, as it will weaken those negative energies and leave them feeling powerless in the space, thus influencing them to leave.

This is exactly why daily spiritual routines are so important. They allow us to cleanse our space and recharge our energies so that we don't create a space that's vulnerable to and habitable for negative energies that can be pesky to get rid of if they're left unattended for too long. Another benefit of daily rituals is that it's simply just a good habit to keep the mind and body in a good rhythm. If we don't have routines within our day, we tend to get lazy and become stuck in stagnant spaces, which can harbor spaces that are inviting for negative, low-vibrational energies. We may start to feel depressed, ill, anxious, worried, paranoid, or unmotivated, which can also leave us feeling powerless. We need to ensure that we are disciplined in our routines so that we stay in spaces (energetically, mentally, emotionally, and physically) that are refreshed and revitalized.

We need to gain a clearer idea of what sort of activities, rituals, or processes we can include in our routine in order to achieve this feeling of being refreshed and revitalized. Daily routines can even include processes as simple as taking a moment to focus on our breathing and meditate. Even affirmations (which have become increasingly popular over the years) are a powerful tool to include in a daily routine.

However, as magick workers, it's our job to draw in and channel energy and manifest that energy and power into our rituals and magick work. Daily routines can also serve as a reminder to magick workers of their special powers. By continuously practicing magick work (through daily routines), a magick worker can also stay in practice and remain strongly connected to the spirit world. Now, with this in mind, we also want to emphasize that daily routines *can* include daily rituals; however, a daily routine for a magick worker doesn't necessarily have to include performing a ritual or spellcasting every single day in order to remain spiritually powerful. The main point, as previously stated, of a daily routine for a magick worker is to remain revitalized and refreshed. Daily routines of magick workers can offer those results (of feeling revitalized) as well as helping the magick worker remain spiritually connected and strong.

Therefore, we refer back to the first aspect that we touched on in this book: *intention*. When we explore practices to include into our daily routine as a magick worker, we want to enter this process with the intention of cleansing the space, which will leave us feeling revitalized. It's important to note that, like adopting any habit, implementing a daily routine will require a lot of motivation and discipline to ensure that we reap the full benefits. If we want to manage energies and work with magick in a sustainable manner, then we need to ensure that we are disciplined with our daily routine.

Finally, as we have come to understand, daily routines are important for our mental, spiritual, emotional, and physical well being. Therefore, anyone can benefit from having routine in their lives. Regular practice of a spiritual routine can offer various benefits to anyone who practices it, regardless of whether the person is a magick worker or not. However, magick workers should treat a spiritual daily routine with more emphasis *because* we are more exposed to energies and spirits.

Creating a Daily Routine

As mentioned above, having a daily routine can benefit anyone and everyone, it doesn't only have to be for magick workers. Spiritual daily routines consist of a set of activities that can help cleanse the space and revitalize our energy sources without even needing to perform any magick work, per sé.

Practices or activities can include things such as lighting a candle, focusing on refining our intention (for the day or on a goal we want to achieve), holding crystals, meditating, spending time in the Sun (which can include drawing, sketching, painting, meditating, or doing yoga in the Sun), using essential oils (such as essential oil roller balls), drawing sigils for good luck, recharging crystals, placing intention in our drinks or food, brewing and drinking herbal teas, to name just a few. There are many other forms of practices to include in our daily routine; however, the most important factor comes down to the intention of the practice: if we performing a daily routine that includes enhancing our intention of rejuvenating ourselves, refreshing our space, recharging our energies, and exercising and enhancing our focus on our intention of our bigger goals, then the daily routine can be deemed good and useful.

Gabriela Herstik, a modern-age (millennial) witch, answered a few questions about being a modern-age witch, in her recent interview with Nylon (Herstik, 2017). In one specific question, Herstik covers the notion of what it means to "stay in practice" as a witch and stray away from the habits of (or lack of) being a "lazy witch." Herstik states that she believes that witches and magick workers have a special, beautiful ability to view the physical world through a 'filtered' reality, whereby they can see the connection between us (in the physical world) and everything else in the universe (spiritually and energetically).

With this in mind, Herstik moves on to say that with this filtered view there is a connection with which magick workers are able to perceive life; and with this notion, we should allow ourselves to go with the ebb and flow of our practice. We shouldn't try to force anything if it doesn't necessarily come to us; magick and energies work on their own agenda, and that isn't a responsibility that we can/should place on ourselves, as it may leave us feeling exhausted or defeated.

Herstik states that staying in practice and avoiding being a 'lazy witch' doesn't necessarily need to include a routine that includes magick work, it simply involves a string of activities to keep one's self grounded and cleansed. Herstik offers a few various activities that she includes in her day-to-day living to help her stay grounded, which include: pulling a tarot card in the morning, taking an intentional photo and setting it as her phone's wallpaper to help her remember the energy or intention of a goal (of which the photo reminds her), asking questions to the Universe or guides and shuffling a deck of tarot cards for guidance, sageing the room or space which she's in, checking on the placement of the Sun and Moon, wearing specific colors to help enhance specific goals or intentions, centering activities or choices of outfits around the Moon phases, meditating in the morning or throughout the day, taking breaks between work to focus on breath work, talking to her guides (which for her, include Venus and Ganesh), and even taking time to talk to or spend time in nature.

Herstik also emphasizes that rearranging your bedroom once in a while can help to clear the space and reshift the energies towards whatever you're manifesting for that period. In terms of prayers, Herstik offers that writing a prayer to our ancestors and lighting a candle can be an intentional and powerful way to remain connected with the spirit world, as well as asking to receive guidance and protection.

All in all, considering Herstik's input, we can gather that our spiritual routine can be extremely broad and creative with the activities we choose to incorporate in our routine. With Herstik's variety of examples in mind of the ways to create a routine, we can take away that our routine doesn't need to be an intense performance inclusive of magick every day: it can be something as simple as spending time in the Sun or even cooking a meal with different herbs. The main goal with our routine is to be intentional with our routine practices.

Finally, Herstik states that as witches and magick workers, we have an innate ability and power to connect with the Universe. Therefore, whatever way we choose to include our routine, we, as magick workers. have the innate ability to make that activity magickal; and with this ability, we are able to remain strongly connected to the energetic world.

Methods to Include in Our Daily Routine

With Herstik affirming our sentiment that routines can include a variety of activities, we can move onto exploring a few good options of activities to include in our daily routine as a magick worker.

Light a Candle

Lighting a candle is one extremely powerful way to remain connected, cleansed, and help enhance your focus and intentions. The simple act of striking a match and lighting a candle alone can be wonderfully empowering as it can help one to center, calm, and ground one's self. Lighting a candle is also extremely quick, resourceful, and can be done at any point in the day. Candles also help create an ambiance that can help one focus more. Choosing the color and scent of a candle can also help to bring in specific energies, trigger specific emotions within us, and help us become much more in tune to the emotions, intentions, and goals we want to achieve.

Magick work usually works well with flames/fire, as magick work is broken up into the three components of intention, energy, and action. Within the process of lighting a candle, we place intention into the lighting of the candle, the action of lighting the candle, and the energy is given off by the flame. Considering this equation, lighting a candle can serve as a way to visibly see the process of magick work (Herstik, 2018).

If you are looking to include lighting a candle as part of your daily routine, and want to reap the magickal benefits that come with the process of candle lighting, then you will want to consider the following two factors: setting your intention and picking the candle and color.

Setting your intention is, will, and should always be the initial step prior to any action, interaction, spell, or ritual. Setting our intention will help us gain a clearer understanding of what we want from the process we're undertaking, and will also help us to attract and manifest the goal, which is established with our intention. Setting our intention when lighting a candle can be as simple as asking ourselves why we are lighting the candle, or it can be a more complex intention, which usually happens when doing spellwork or rituals.

When working with candles for magick work, you will want to first ask yourself whether you're trying to attract or banish something within the magick work you're about to perform. Establishing this factor will greatly help you to further create an atmosphere around that intention of attracting something or protecting and banishing something: this energy and atmosphere is then enhanced and manifested by the candle's flame. If you have a specific goal or spell that you'd like to enhance and use the candle's flame as energy to manifest that goal, then one way to do this is to write that intention on a piece of paper and place it close to the lit candle; leave it there as the candle burns. Alternatively, others recite a chant or meditate while the candle burns, which can also help to enhance whatever intention/goal you would like to manifest or banish.

Second, choosing the type of candle and color of the candle can also help to specify the intention of the spell or ritual. Even if you're not planning on doing magick work and simply want to light a candle to center yourself, choosing a candle and color can help you to keep your space cleansed and protected. We can refer back to the previous chapter to explore what colors symbolize and how they enhance different intentions. This information can also be applied when choosing the color of the candle. For instance, if you'd like to work with candles for a banishing spell or ritual, then black candles can be used to enhance the intention and atmosphere needed to banish that spirit, curse, or energy.

Lighting a Candle (Kyejo, 2020)

Similarly, this notion can be applied for different colors that symbolize different intentions and goals. However, if you cannot find different colored candles, you can use any candle, it's not that important in the grand scheme of things. Choosing a colored candle that aligns with the symbolism and intention of the spell or ritual will just help enhance the energies more, but if you cannot get a hold of a specific color, then any color can be used. Ideally speaking, white candles are best suited for magick work if you can't find a specific color, as white candles are generic and can be used for and symbolize anything.

Holding a Crystal

> We can use crystals to identify, raise and direct energy to a targeted source.
> —Faragher & Saint Thomas, 2018

Holding a crystal can also serve as an extremely powerful and effective way to recharge our own energies. It's also resourceful and isn't time consuming, as we can hold crystals while we meditate, place them under our pillow when we sleep, wear them as jewelry, or simply keep them around our space.

Choosing our crystals is similar to choosing colors of candles: different crystals symbolize and attract different energies, which can then be used to help us manifest our intentions. As a magick worker, we tend to work very closely with crystals as they offer powerful energies and can serve as powerful tools to use within our own spells and rituals. Therefore, it's not uncommon to see a witch, warlock, or spiritual healer with a set of crystals near them or their spaces. Building a good, strong set of crystals is an important step in any beginner magick worker's journey.

What's even more interesting and amazing about crystals is that they can store energy within them and recharge their own energy levels (essentially serving as conductors). Specific crystals can then be used for specific energies, intentions, or magick work. The more charged those specific crystals are, the more powerful they can be to draw out that energy or attract an energy we are calling upon.

To provide a quick breakdown, black tourmaline stones can be used for protection, baby pink rose quartz stones can be used to call upon self-love, and bright yellow citrine crystals can be used for attracting abundance.

In addition to the type and color of crystals, it's also believed that the shapes of crystals matter. The geometric structural shapes of the crystals determine how the crystal energy flows through the stones to produce different forms of energies. Crystals also have parallels with the fundamental notions of spellwork, as crystals essentially help to generate energy, then identify and raise that vibrational energy, and thereafter, redirect that energy to a specific target (such as an intention or goal within our magick work). Crystals also have the ability to mirror our power; therefore, when we charge crystals with direct intentions, they can work independently to manifest that energy.

When working with crystals, you will need to reset its vibrations by washing it with water, saging the crystal, or placing it under the light of the full Moon. Once the crystal is reset, hold it within your hands, close your eyes, and think of your intention with your crystal. You can then repeat that intention by manifesting the intention with a chant or visualization; this will help the crystal to absorb the energy from the intention. Continue with this process until you feel that the energetic transfer to the crystal is complete.

Thereafter, you can keep the crystal near you or in a specific space, such as your bedroom or under your pillow. Some magick workers prefer to only take their crystals out and use them during rituals, while others prefer to keep the crystals with them throughout the day. This decision is completely up to you and how you would like to use your crystals.

In terms of choosing the crystals, many magick workers say that they feel as though they don't choose the crystal, but rather the crystal chooses them. This simply suggests that we allow our intuition to choose the crystals. This process also allows us to trust our intuition to see which crystals and energies will help us the most. If you're planning on buying crystals in a store, you can also focus on the intention you'd like to manifest in the chosen crystal, and then try to hold different crystals in your palms to see which crystals give off more powerful energetic pulls. For example, if you set your intention and hold different crystals with that intention in mind, you may feel that some crystals will leave your palms feeling hotter (this can be from a strong energy transfer) or some crystals may leave you feeling more tranquil. The crystals that you hold that leave you feeling a stronger energetic connection can be the crystals best suited for you and your intention; thus, those crystals can be a few of your top choices.

If you are looking to acquire crystals online, one can still focus in on the intention that you would like to place in a crystal, and then choose a crystal based off of the crystal/mineral that best matches your intention.

For those who are just starting out with their crystal collection, building a crystal collection can seem overwhelming at first, especially when one is still learning about the properties of crystals and how they work. Therefore, a few fantastic crystals to collect when starting off are clear quartz, amethyst, rose quartz, citrine, and black tourmaline (Faragher & Saint Thomas, 2018). These five crystals are both powerful crystals to possess, easily accessible, and affordable, making them perfect choices for starting off a crystal collection.

Clear quartz is a crystal known for its healing capabilities through an increase in positive vibrations. The clear quartz is, as its name intends, clear in color. Many tend to also refer to the clear quartz as the "master healer" as this crystal is a fantastic choice for its healing properties. The clear quartz is a fantastic all-round, all-purpose type of crystal to possess, as it can be used to generally raise positive vibrations of any positive intentions. It is also easy to use, as one can simply hold it in their hands and concentrate on their intention or the goal that they'd like to place in the crystal (it can be a specific goal or a general, broad goal, such as inviting love, healing, or abundance into one's life). Thereafter, this process can be incorporated into a magick worker's daily routine or used during spellwork, rituals, or meditation and manifestation work.

Amethyst is another popular crystal to possess. It's best known for its distinctive purple color and is best used to help magick workers enhance their psychic powers, reach a higher state of consciousness, and provide protection by warding off negative energies from a space. Amethyst is also best known and used for its healing properties, which is why it can often be worn as a necklace or placed near someone's heart during periods of sadness or anxiousness. Amethysts are believed to help provide healing for psychological pain and the crystal is perceived as a powerful tool to clear low-vibrational energies within a space; therefore, it's seen as a precious crystal to give to those during periods of grief, heartache, or emotional distress. As the amethyst crystal can help promote psychic powers and help those using the crystal to tap into a higher state of consciousness, we can also use the crystal to enhance our dream state and even dream recall, when keeping the crystal nearby. This process can also help further enhance our psychic abilities within our dreams.

Rose quartz crystals give off a gorgeous, light peach color. This crystal (as with the color) symbolizes and helps enhance love, compassion, harmony, and beauty. Rose quartz can help one welcome in a new romance or help heal any existing relationship troubles. The crystal promotes extremely tranquil, soothing, and peaceful emotions; therefore, the crystal can be used to help us heal and open our hearts to embrace love, passion, and intimacy. In addition to this, rose quartz can be used to help those who are going through a grieving period, one especially related to the mourning of a lover who has passed on, or even mourning a relationship that has ended. Finally, rose quartz can also promote any other positive vibrational energies affiliated with the heart chakra; this includes opening ourselves up to greater intimacy, gaining a better sense of self-love, and even bettering friendships.

Citrine is known for its distinctive golden color, thus making it a crystal that's powerful for energies related to optimism, creativity, and prosperity. Citrine is a fantastic crystal to work with, for those who want to work more with manifestation magic. If you want to work with crystals to manifest opportunities, prosperity, happiness, and abundance, then citrine crystals are a powerful tool to use. Citrine can be used by placing it in the sunlight to absorb the light and charge its powers. Thereafter, citrine crystals can be held in our palms or worn in jewelry pieces for us (or our loved ones) to absorb the intentions and manifestations which we placed within the crystal.

Citrine (Staab, 2018)

Citrine is also a powerful crystal that promotes greater self-confidence, self-worth, and self-respect. Citrine is also believed to help attract more money because it helps you to realize your self-worth and self-confidence much more. In essence, citrine can help us to manifest and attract material abundance (if that is our intention) by helping fuel energy and power into realizing and heightening our own sense of self. Citrine helps us reach more powerful and positive stages in our life, whereby we are able to confidently dream, manifest, attract, and deserve abundance in our lives. Citrine doesn't only offer physical (material) transformation, but also mental and emotional transformation.

Finally, black tourmaline is a fantastic crystal to promote spiritual protection. Black tourmaline, as the name suggests, is black in color. It works as a powerful protection tool by absorbing in any negative energies and emitting positive energies, thus serving as a force-field protector, in a sense. With this in mind, many tend to wear black tourmaline as a jewelry piece to help protect them, while others prefer to keep a black tourmaline either in their work or home space, or even carry a black tourmaline in their pocket, handbag, or attached to their key ring. We will also be covering more crystals in detail in Chapter 5: Protection Idols and Amulets.

Standing Sun Salutation

Another powerful practice that many magick workers like to include in their daily routine is the Standing Sun Salutation. In simple terms, the Standing Sun Salutation is essentially a basic yoga pose that helps one reconnect with Mother Nature, which can then help us feel calm, reconnected, grounded, present, and aware (Stewart, n.d.). However, magick workers can take the Standing Sun Salutation and gain many more benefits from this practice, as we can use this pose as a way to draw upon strong, powerful and positive energies. In doing so, we can ground ourselves and be energetically prepared for the magick work which we need to perform throughout the day.

The Standing Sun Salutation can be done in a 5-minute daily practice, making it a resourceful practice to perform. It is performed by first finding a spot in the Sun (preferably during sunrise or sunset). Stand upright, barefoot, and face the Sun. Close your eyes and focus on your feet contacting the earth (grounding yourself) and then move onto focusing on your breathing. Inhale deeply and raise your arms above your head, having your palms facing towards each other but not touching. Upon exhalation, lower your arms back down and bring them into prayer pose. From there, inhale once more and "float over in a standing forward bend" (yoga pose), then exhale slowly. Inhale once again and raise your head and heart halfway, then exhale and allow yourself to hang downwards (Stewart, n.d.). Finally, inhale once more and lift your hands above your head (in the same manner as the first position) and then exhale, bringing your hands to prayer pose.

The Standing Sun Salutation is best done when standing in the Sun during sunrise or sunset, however it can be performed anywhere. If you are indoors and want to face towards the Sun when performing this stance, then that can also be beneficial. The most important factor to consider when performing the Standing Sun Salutation is that you need to focus your intention on feeling grounded, positive, and calm during this process. You should focus on feeling the positive and re-energizing energies flowing through you. As you inhale and exhale during this ritual, you try to be aware of the energetic flow as you breathe.

Essential Oil Roller Ball

Making use of an essential oil roller ball can also be extremely beneficial, as it can calm us down, enhance our focus and even help us become more grounded and present in the moment. Essential oil roller balls are both resourceful and handy to keep around, as they can be carried anywhere. You can choose which fragrance (essential oil) you'd like to keep around with you. Simply fill your roller ball with your essential oil of choice and then, whenever you need a little help calming down or focusing, apply a little oil on your wrists, neck, or behind your ears. Allow the oils to sit on the skin, do not rub it in. This will help the scent of the oil to be potent and strong, which can serve as the most powerful and efficient way to help you feel better.

Drawing Sigils

Drawing sigils is another powerful practice to include in a daily routine if you enjoy working with symbols, signs, sigils, and other similar practices that can serve as protection, positive vibrations, or good luck. Drawing sigils are also another extremely quick, easy, and resourceful way to call upon and draw good energy without needing too many resources or time. Drawing sigils can be done with anything around us; it can even be creatively done by drawing a small symbol/sigil within your container of face cream, or drawn with jam onto your morning toast! This can help us to understand that we can draw upon the intention of that energy (represented by the sigil) at any point in our day; it can be done at any time, anywhere.

The primary benefit of sigils (apart from it being extremely accessible) is that it allows us to hone in on focusing on and drawing in good luck and good energy at any point in the day (Caro, 2020a). Including sigils in our daily practice can also fall under practicing the law of attraction, as it helps us to be more conscious about our intentions and, thus, be more clear of our intentions and goals that we want to attract.

Ideally sigils should be done in the morning, as this will help us to set our focus and intentions for the day ahead. Drawing sigils first thing in the morning will also help us move into the right frame of mind (needed to attract the energies required for our intention), as well as help us maneuver through our day in alignment with our intention which we placed in the sigil.

One of the most powerful and most common of sigils to draw upon is the good luck sigil. This sigil helps us to raise our energies to a higher vibration as well as attract more positive energies that we want to fuel into an intention/ goal of ours. We can even use a good luck sigil as a form of protection: for instance, if something isn't going in the right direction, we can draw a good luck sigil for more positive luck and energy.

Drawing a sigil starts with an intention or goal which you would like the sigil to direct positive energy into: the more precise and straightforward the desire, the more powerful the sigil. Take this goal or intention (usually a positive affirmation) and turn it into a present-tense sentence. For example, instead of saying "I will be healthy," say "I *am* healthy." Next, write this affirmation on a piece of paper in order to first create the sigil, then delete any repeating alphabets within the word/phrase. So, for instance, "I will be healthy" will leave you with the letters *I*, *w*, *l*, *b*, *e*, *h*, *a*, *t*, *h*, and *y*.

The next step is where we get creative: take the letters and connect them into an abstract symbol. You can connect the letters by the lines and curves of each letter to create the sigil. If you're unhappy with the first attempt, you can try it as many times until you're happy with the symbol. Thereafter, you can use this sigil in your daily practice, drawing it wherever and whenever you please. It's important to remember, however, that when you do draw your sigil, you remember to focus on the intention and goal behind the sigil.

A Cup of Tea

Another powerful and considerably common practice which can help us calm down, reground ourselves, and even enhance our levels of concentration is to simply pour a cup of tea. Pouring and having a cup of tea is extremely powerful, especially considering that there are a variety of herbal tea options that serve different purposes. Some herbal teas can help us to concentrate, while other teas calm us down and help us reground ourselves, and other teas can serve healing/medicinal purposes! Therefore, collecting a good variety of herbal teas can also help us as magick workers to remain grounded, calm, and focused.

Additionally, the process of making and brewing tea is also considered a spiritual process, as it influences us to be present in the moment and can be an extremely calming process. Choosing the mug can also be a powerful moment, as we can be intentional and conscious about what choice of mug we would like to use. There's also a sense of affirming the power we possess by knowing that we have the power to choose our mug, of which, the mug can also serve as a further affirmation for the day. For example, if you choose a mug with an affirmative saying on it, or if it has specific colors or symbols, then we can treat these choices in a mug as more of an affirmation for the day. Choosing a mug is a very personal and powerful experience, as the beverage which you're pouring into the mug is treated as a physical form of the intention that the mug is portraying (Klug, 2020). For instance, if you choose a yellow mug that has a sun and a saying along the lines of "have a good day," then the tea which we drink from the mug can serve as a physical/ritual form of the intention of having a good, a happy day.

Thereafter, choosing the right type of tea requires asking how you are feeling and what you need the tea to do: for example, does the tea need to help you focus or calm down? There are a variety of herbal teas with different purposes, so try to hone in on what you and your body need, and then question how your choice in mug and tea can help that. You can even question what your goals or tasks of the day are, and then choose your mug and tea accordingly.

Next, preparing the tea properly is extremely important: this includes brewing the tea. Some teas require 7 to 10 minutes of brewing, while other teas only require 3 minutes. This factor is extremely important in the tea-brewing process as this determines how strong and effective the tea is. If you do enjoy more herbalist rituals, one can even grow, pick, and grind their own medicinal mixtures of teas.

Once the tea is properly brewed, consider how you best enjoy your tea and what requirements that specific tea will need. For example, some teas (such as rooty teas) work best when decocted in water, while other teas (such as matcha tea, for instance) work best when the tea is whisked and frothed. This process is a combination of your preferences and what works best with each tea.

Tea rituals also include time for blending the tea, steeping it, stirring it, smelling it, brewing it, and so forth. There are so many beautiful steps in tea making that can really help benefit us and bring us to a calmer and more grounded state. Choosing how elaborate you'd like your tea ritual to be is completely up to your own personal preferences and what you would like to benefit from the tea making and drinking process.

With the above daily ritual practices in mind, we can see how truly vast the practices are and how we can be as creative and personal as we would like, in order to create a routine that's personalized and effective for us. We can also take away that daily routine practices also don't require a lot of spellwork or magic, but rather practices that are resourceful and easily accessible, which then help us to manage our spellwork much more efficiently. These daily routines help us, as magick workers, ensure that we are looking after ourselves so that we can handle the magick work we do in a more responsible and safe manner! With the above routine examples in mind, do you have your daily routine in place? And if so, are you practicing the art of being consciously present, aware and intentional with your routine? This is what we need to ensure that we aim for, every day!

Techniques for Protection

As we have come to understand thus far, protection is important for every single one of us. However, protection is *especially* important for those actively practicing in the field of magick.

Magick workers are constantly exposed to all sorts of energies, people, and spirits on a daily basis, and it's our duty as magick workers to ensure that balance is restored in areas where there is energetic disruption.

Considering the above, this exposure can be extremely energetically taxing on a magick worker. One way to ensure that we maintain some form of balance and stability in our life is to ensure that we're following a disciplined daily routine. In doing so, we are ensuring that our own levels of energy are recharged for the day ahead. A daily routine is vital for us to feel prepared for the day's work ahead. Additionally, clearing our space of any pesky negative energies can also be done more easily when protection and our cleansing rituals are incorporated into our daily routine.

In this chapter, we are going to be exploring a few of the most common and key ways to protect ourselves on a daily basis, as well as a few ways to protect ourselves prior to performing magick work.

The Vital Importance of Radiating

Radiating in magick work is one of the most powerful forms of protection we can possess and practice. Radiating is powerful because it can be performed daily and incorporated into our way of life, and the more we practice something, the more powerful we become in that aspect.

With this in mind, the practice of radiating is simply practicing radiating positive energy. When we practice radiating, we become forcefully powerful in diminishing any negative energies, thus leaving those energies feeling hostile and exiting from our space. Radiating plays on the aspect that what we give attention to is what we attract and give power to. Therefore, if we want to only attract positive energy (or even cleanse ourselves and our space from negative energy), then we must focus on the practice of radiating positive energy.

Radiating is also a powerful tool to use to help us simply maneuver through life with much more ease. By practicing the art of radiating positive energy, we constantly train ourselves (even subconsciously) to find the positive attributes, experiences, resources, and solutions to events we face on a daily basis. Radiating positivity will not only completely reform our own thought patterns, but it will also help us to realize the power of intention. When we reform our mindsets to one that is positive, we start to protect ourselves and our space from any obstacles and negative energies. We, ourselves, become unattractive to negative energies because that positive radiation becomes so overwhelmingly powerful in the face of negativity.

Now, the above sentiment may seem to be a bit of a rollercoaster to understand, especially considering how radiating protection techniques work into our subconscious to affect our physical well being; however, it can be simply understood that practicing the protection technique of radiating positive energy will help us create an unattractive environment for negative energies, thus allowing us to create and exist in a protected space.

Radiating positive energy and protection spellwork and magick work hand-in-hand with one another to create a positive and protected space. We need positive energy to help shield us from negativity, and we need protection to help us create spaces of positive energy.

With the above sentiment in mind, we can move on to explore a few of the main techniques that help us to call upon and radiate positivity: *clearing* and *manifesting*.

Clearing the Space

> While clearing, you should have a mantra like, "I replace any negative energy in this space with my highest and best energy." Finish by setting an intention for clear communication.
> —Erica Feldman (Garis, 2020)

The element of clearing a magick worker's space should be treated as an ultimate priority for any magick worker who is in practice, especially if you're dealing with multiple people, energies, or spirits on a daily basis.

Think about it this way: if you go to a doctor's office, it's important that their area, the medical tools and the surgical chair are cleaned after each patient's visit. This is to ensure that no illness is spread to other patients, and also to ensure that the doctor and their staff are safe. A clean working space is essential for a business or profession to function. Similarly, when we acquire crystals, we also need to cleanse them before and after using them.

Therefore, with this in mind, we need to also ensure that we energetically and physically keep our space cleansed. Erica Feldman, a modern-day witch, suggests that we can also focus on energetically charging our cleaning supplies by holding them and meditating with them with the intention of the cleaning supplies assisting in cleaning the space both physically and energetically.

Thereafter, smudging can also be an effective way to energetically cleanse the space. The most common herb that people use to burn and smudge is sage; however, other herbs, such as cedar, mugwort, or various other cleansing herbs can be used. There are also other alternatives with herbs, such as sage spray, which you can purchase or make at home.

Other forms of cleansing a space can include ringing bells, banging drums, using sound bowls, humming, playing meditation music (such as different hertz vibrational songs; this can even be found on Youtube), clapping your hands, dancing, creating a beat in general, or playing positive vibrational music. Feldman states that any form of cleansing is good, as long as it's intention is to replace any negative energy in a space with your highest and most positive energy. Thereafter, Feldman likes to end her cleanse by setting a specific intention in the space to ensure that there's clear communication during her practices.

Manifesting

Manifesting has definitely become an increasingly popular practice over the past few years; it has also been a common practice for many who want to visualize and attract what they would like to achieve or acquire in their life. Manifestations also help us to gain a clearer idea of what we truly want, help us to place greater focus on what we want, and then attract and embrace what we want.

For magick workers, the practice of manifestation extends much further than simply visualizing and attracting what we want to achieve. Manifestation can help us to attract positive energies and, in turn, radiate positive energy and protect our space. Therefore, with this in consideration, we can take away that manifestation can be used as another form of radiating positive energy and, thus, serving as another way to protect ourselves and our space. We can use the power of manifestation to also expand on our positive energy and ensure that the space we're in is one of abundance and filled with endless blessings.

Manifestation, like meditation, can be done in numerous ways and is all up to the individual's preference. If you prefer a more ritualistic and physical approach to manifestation, then you could include signs, sigils, objects, idols, and so forth to create alters, jars, scrapbooks, or even an amulet as a form of manifestation. Alternatively, others tend to prefer more verbal forms of manifestations, which include chants, reciting spells, and even affirmations. Lastly, another popular option of manifestation is to practice it internally, similar to practices such as meditation and visualizations. You can also work with crystals (with any of the manifestation methods) to draw upon the energy or transfer your intention into the crystals.

Whichever method of manifestation you prefer to practice, it's important to ensure that you maintain the same level of intention and focus with your process. This is why the actual method of manifestation isn't as important and can be left up to the manifestor's preferences, as this comes secondary to the importance of the intention and focus required. As a magick worker, trusting your intuition is extremely important as it can greatly help enhance your powers when you work in alignment with that intuition. Therefore, using intuition to see which method of manifestation works best can greatly help you tap into a more powerful state with enhanced magick powers, thus allowing you to reap more effective and powerful benefits from your manifestations.

SHIELDING YOURSELF

After the process and practice of radiating is done, we can also consider the next form of protection: shields. Shields are essentially energy barriers that we can craft to protect ourselves from any energetic threats. Shields can be crafted regardless of your situation, and you don't necessarily need to know or experience a negative energy or threat in order to craft a shield: you can craft a shield at any point in the day for any occasion.

Crafting a shield can even be done as a precautionary measure, simply for the sake of having it.

Crafting a personal protection shield can be compared to essentially having a second layer of skin, but this second layer is an energetic layer that serves as protection from negative energies and threats which you may be exposed to throughout the day. Magick workers may also want to craft a personal shield when they are casting spellwork or performing rituals without casting a circle of protection first.

Personal shields can also be crafted if you feel a sudden drop in energy levels, a wave of depression, sudden/drastic changes in mood or attitude, a wave of uneasiness, or a wave of anxiety or stress. These are a few side effects that can suggest that negative energy is coming towards you, around you, or attempting to attach itself to you. A few other reasons to craft a shield is if you feel drained after a social gathering; if you feel tired, lethargic, or exhausted all-day; if you feel intense emotional or psychic exhaustion; if you find yourself constantly replaying conversations or encounters in your head; if you find yourself struggling to let go of events that agitate or upset you, to list a few. Crafting shields can help you to speed up your emotional and psychic healing, while also helping you to recharge your energy shields and refocus your attention on radiating that positive energy.

With this in mind, crafting shields are generally done by visualizing an energy barrier that covers you from head to toe. There are two main types of shield spells, known as the *personal shield spell* and the *advanced shield spell*. Explaining these will allow us to go into more detail of the specific processes required for crafting a shield spell.

The Personal Shield Spell

The personal shield spell is, as the name states, a shield that can be crafted for one's self. This shield can be crafted at any point in the day and for any occasion. The personal shield spell is also considered the basic shield spell, or first step rather, to perform in order to perform more advanced magick and spell-work. For example, if we want to craft shields to extend beyond ourselves and our space, we will want to first craft a personal shield spell in order to ensure that we're protected enough to perform further magic.

A personal shield spell is crafted by first closing your eyes and grounding yourself: this is done by focusing on the flow of the energy moving from the Earth and through your body. Focus on the sensations that come with the energy flowing through your body, such as a tingling sensation, the warmth of the energy, and the calming effect which comes with the energy flow.

As the energy flows through your body, try to call upon the Earth's positive energy and draw that energy towards your core. Thereafter, start to visualize that the energy starts to expand until it covers your entire body, and then expands around the outside of your body so as to create a bubble of a shield. Try to ensure that your bubble/shield is as small as possible and as close to your skin as possible, because the bigger and further the bubble is from your body, the harder it is to control and maintain (Hawthorn, 2021).

While visualizing the energy forming a bubble around you, you can also include using chants to help you focus on and visualize the shield, such as "I am safe within my shield" or "I am protected by my shield." You can also make use of crystals, or meditation music, or even lighting incense to help you calm down and focus your attention on visualizing and manifesting the personal protection shield.

This personal protection shield can be included in your daily routine to prepare you for each day, or it can be done every so often, or simply be done prior to working with magick. Either way, your intuition will be able to tell you when and how often you will need to craft a shield.

The Advanced Shield Spell

The advanced shield spell is, as the name suggests, a level up from the personal protection shield spell. It requires much more time, effort, power, and experience to ensure that this spell works properly.

As previously stated in the personal shield spell, when we extend our personal shield further from our body, it becomes much more difficult to control and maintain. This is where the advanced shield spell comes into play: this spell can help us to visualize the personal protective shield as a stronger material than a bubble of a shield.

The advanced shield spell works with the same steps as the personal protective shield spell; however, we aim to visualize the advanced shield spell with a much stronger material, such as glass, metal, or a mirror. The choice of this material is entirely up to you, your ability to craft and visualize that material, and what material you feel safest being protected by. For instance, crafting a shield out of mirror or glass can be effective as it can deflect all negative energies that may want to come towards you. In addition to this, negative energies will also have a tougher time identifying you as you're 'cloaked' in a sense, by a reflective shield.

DeFlecting: Absorbing or Returning Spells, Curses, or Hexes

Building off of the previous section on the benefits of an advanced shield spell, the practice of deflection works in a similar manner, whereby we deflect any negative energy that's entering our path or being directed towards us.

Returning involves the process of deflecting any curses, spells, or hexes that may come your way, and this form of protective magick can be extremely beneficial, especially for those of us who actively work with magick on a day-to-day basis.

On the other hand, some prefer the alternative to returning, which is to absorb energy into objects instead. We usually tend to see this form of deflection take place with magick jars, boxes, and sachéts that contain items that are sympathetic and have absorbed negative energies. These items are then stored away in a unit (such as a jar or a box) which is then blessed so as to ensure that the energies are not tampered with or rereleased into the world.

Some tend to work with sympathetic items that absorb energy, such as poppets or dolls, while others tend to craft energy into other items, such as charms, herbs, or crystals that can then be stowed away or cleansed after absorbing the energies.

A few herbs that can absorb energies well include rosemary, basil, cinnamon, clove, ginger, sage, bay leaf, black pepper, and cumin (Hawthorn, 2021). These herbs can be placed into a pouch and then you can craft the pouch to draw in any negative energy in the surrounding areas.

If you prefer using crystals to absorb energy, or would like to include crystals in your sachét or jar, a few good choices of crystals are black tourmaline, obsidian, smokey quartz, labradorite, and amethyst.

Once you fill a pouch, jar, or sachét with items that you've crafted to absorb any negative energies, you can then carry this pouch with you wherever you go as a form of protection, or you can leave it in your home or workplace to simply keep your space cleansed and protected.

Whether you choose to craft a personal shield, deflect, or craft items to absorb negative energy is all up to your own personal preferences. Some magick workers prefer to deflect energies, while others feel as though absorbing negative energies works better for them. The choice of which type of protection you'd like to use is entirely up to you as well as the energies you're dealing with. For instance, sometimes deflection will work for some energies while absorption will work on other energies.

CLOAKING

When thinking of cloaking, I instantly think back to Harry Potter's cloak of invisibility. Interestingly enough, we are also able to create our own cloaks of invisibility! Similar to the notion of a deflective advanced shield (made of glass or mirror), cloaking can serve as a way for us to work with magick while seeming 'invisible' to negative energies that want to attach onto us.

In doing so, cloaking allows us to, in a way, be protected from energies while we go about our magick work.

Cloaking is an extremely simple, powerful, and resourceful way to protect ourselves. The steps are as follows: first start by grounding and centering yourself. This step can be done through meditation or focusing on breathwork. If you need tea or crystals to assist with this process of calming down and grounding yourself, then these can also be used.

Once you've centered yourself, visualize yourself in a luminous, angelic white light. Focus on this light and visualize it surrounding your entire body, literally *cloaking* yourself in it. Once the light surrounds you, feel your body's density start to dissipate and merge with the white light. All the elements that make your physical, dense body are now immersed in the soft white light and becoming one with it. Your skin, flesh, muscle, blood, bones, hair, all start to dissolve into this overpowering, all-encompassing white light.

Once you feel the process is complete and you're cloaked, end the spell with this chant: "Cloak of invisibility, I now decree, protect and guard and shield me" (Parma, 2014).

Now, with the above protection tools, we can cover ourselves as magick workers in various aspects of life. Whether we want to simply radiate positive energy, cleanse the space and manifest (which can all be included in daily routines if one pleases) to more advanced, powerful, and intentional forms of protection, such as crafting a protection shield, deflecting or cloaking ourselves, we can ensure that we can peacefully and responsibly carry on with our day as a magick worker and know that we are protected and guarded by good energy in the magick world.

In terms of choosing which types of protection techniques you would like to use, it's entirely up to you, the energies you're exposed to, the magick you're dealing with, and what you feel is necessary. As previously stated, one of the most powerful tools we have as magick workers is our intuition. Aim to trust your intuition to guide you on how much protection, cleansing, radiating, deflecting, or cloaking you will need. In addition to this, you will also need to consider what type of energy and magick you're dealing with to determine how much protection you will need.

Protection Objects and Idols

As we have come to see in the past two chapters especially, refining our routine and practice as a magick worker is extremely intricate and reliant on intention. There are, however, a variety of items that are believed to possess specific magickal properties, such as different crystals, herbs, colored candles, and so forth. Therefore, if we want to be more intentional and effective with our magick work, we can incorporate such items in our practice.

One of the most notable takeaways from the previous chapter are the processes of absorption and deflection. We can directly link and apply these processes to the subject of protection idols and objects. In this chapter, we are going to be exploring a few of the most commonly used objects, crystals, and even herbs used for protection. We will also explore the notion of how these items can be used to either absorb or deflect negative energy, and the best way to use them.

Amulets, symbols, crystals, and herbs have been used in medicinal and magick work for centuries, spanning across various traditions and cultures. To this day, various magick workers across the world hold similar beliefs in the magickal properties of the items we are going to explore, and actively use these items for spiritual and energetic protection.

Whether we use the items for magick work or to simply include them in our daily routine (for instance, including herbs in our tea), we can greatly benefit from the magickal benefits of these items.

PROTECTION AMULETS

Protection amulets can essentially be understood as items that have been crafted by a magick worker and serve a specific intention and purpose, an intention that was placed in the amulet by the magick worker.

In regards to 'types' of amulets, they can be divided into three categories. The first type of an amulet is used to attract and then divert malevolent gaze, such as an evil eye amulet. The second type of amulet is worn in secrecy (usually as or with an undergarment) and kept as a secret. The third type of an amulet is the type to be written on paper/parchment and kept within a small box, jar, or locket and carried with you at all times. The amulet symbols that we are going to explore within this section can come in the form of any of the three types. For example, a ladybug amulet can be worn as an accessory, in an undergarment, or written on a piece of parchment and carried with you.

While we can use various different objects and items as amulets (such as our own personal 'good luck charm,' for instance), there are a few noteworthy amulet symbols that serve specific purposes and help with specific intentions. Similar to the notion that different colored candles help enhance and attract different, specific intentions, the same applies with amulets and their symbols. While we can place intention into any given object, there are a few amulets with specific symbols that can assist us in manifesting specific things with greater ease.

A few amulet symbols are the ladybug, horn, horseshoe, cat, and cricket amulets; however, there are many other symbols which you can explore for various other purposes (Caro, 2020b). These five, however, are specific to providing protection.

The Ladybug Amulet

First on the list is the ladybug amulet. Ladybugs are believed to symbolize good luck. The belief goes that if a ladybug is placed on your hand, it means that good luck will come your way. However many dots on the ladybug's red elytra equate to the amount of months you will surely receive good luck. If the ladybug can stay on your hand long enough for you to count to 22, then this means that the luck it brings will be even greater.

If the ladybug flies or lands on you by itself, then this means that it is bringing luck and fortune your way. As this is the belief that is affiliated with ladybugs, we see similar symbolic and energetic ties to ladybug amults. Many love to wear ladybug charms or amulets to attract similar good luck and fortune into their lives.

Ladybug (Myriams, 2016)

The Horn Amulet

The horn symbol has been a symbol of good luck and fertility for centuries, throughout various cultures and traditions. The horn amulet has also served as a lucky charm in southern Italy, where it's worn and used as a way to protect its wearer from the evil eye, envy, and any form of directed negative energy.

The origin of the beliefs that come with the horn as a symbol of luck, fertility, and protection is somewhat vague; however, many believe that the horn shape is derived from the cornucopia, which are goat horns filled with gold and other precious minerals from the earth. Many believe that the cornucopia is a symbol of abundance, and thus, this may have been translated into many believing in the symbolism of the horn amulet.

Many also share the belief that when one turns the horn amulet with the index finger and little finger, it can shift the evil eye away from the holder of the horn amulet.

The most classic color for the horn amulet is red, and it is vitally important that the horn amulet is handmade. If you buy a real horn or one that is not handmade, this can bring negative energies towards you. However, if you have received a horn amulet as a gift or found it, this amulet can serve as an amulet of protection against envy, jealousy, and the evil eye.

The Horseshoe Amulet

The horseshoe symbol has got to be one of the most popularly known lucky charms, as well as one of the most effective. The belief in the horseshoe symbol and amulet dates back to ancient legends from England, and primarily stems down to the belief that the horseshoe's piece of iron can ward off negative energies and evil spirits.

There have also been traces of the horseshoe found in ancient Rome, and it's believed that they once used the horseshoe amulet as a way to protect themselves from the plague. During the Middle Ages, doctors also used the horseshoe amulet as a way of healing the sick.

If the horseshoe amulet is hanging anywhere (such as on a wall or on a necklace), it's essential that it is hanging with its ends facing upwards, with the rounded edge facing downwards. This is believed to be the only way that the horseshoe's powers will work and be effective.

If one is working with an actual animal's horseshoe, it has to first be worn by the animal before it can possess any effective powers. Thereafter, the horseshoe can be touched to bring about luck and good fortune. There is, however, a popular myth that states that if the horseshoe comes from one of the animals' rear hooves, then it can bring about bad luck.

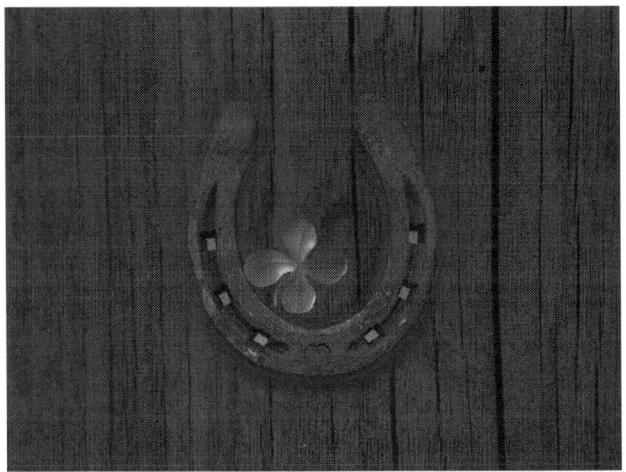

Horseshoe (Kalhh, 2016)

The Cat Amulet

The symbolism of the cat also dates back to ancient times in various cultures and traditions. Ancient Egypt, for instance, worshipped the cat as a powerful, sacred animal. East Asian cultures also valued the cat, especially when represented with one of its paws raised; this was believed to ward away evil spirits. In addition to this, it's believed that cats were blessed with various magickal and psychic powers.

With this in mind, the cat amulet can be worn as an accessory or placed as an amulet in the home or work space. It's mainly used for its purposes to protect the home and family in space, as the cat symbolizes (and is believed to) be a protecting spirit.

Lucky Cat (Burke, 2018)

The Cricket Amulet

Another amulet that symbolizes luck and good fortune is the cricket. It's believed that the cricket amulet can simultaneously dispel misfortune while also attracting good fortune and luck. There is also a popular belief that if a person of pure soul captures a cricket, it will have to fulfill a wish for them.

Crickets are also believed to be a symbol of luck and can ensure a promising gain of wealth. If you hear crickets around your home or near you, it's believed to be a good omen and a sign of good luck coming your way.

PROTECTION CRYSTALS

Similar to amulets, crystals can also possess various benefits and can help protect us as well as attract good energies when worn or used. As we have come to understand with crystals thus far, they are extremely useful tools for magick workers as we can use crystals for various purposes within our spellwork.

Crystals, like amulets, also possess specific symbolism, powers, and beliefs attached to them. We can also carry crystals around with us (as pieces of jewelry) or keep them in our homes to protect our space and attract good energy. Similar to the symbolism of color within our spellwork and rituals, different crystals also possess different, specific qualities that help us maneuver through life with more ease, protection, and good omens. It's important that we explore the different, specific purposes with each crystal so as to ensure that we are working as efficiently as possible with crystals.

Crystals, for a magick worker, are one of the most effective and powerful tools to use. This is why it's always advised that beginner magick workers start collecting a few powerful crystals and familiarize themselves and their work with the different crystals. We, as magick workers, can greatly benefit from the use of crystals. We can use crystals to cleanse spaces, absorb negative energy and transform it into positive energy, conduct and direct energy towards different things, recharge our energy levels, heal people or situations, use crystals for manifestation work ... the list is truly endless!

Within this section, we are going to explore a few of the most common/popular crystals used for protection and attracting good energy. We will also explore how best to use these crystals in our daily life to ensure that we're using the right crystal for its intended purpose, and thus, reaping the most powerful effects from it.

Clear Quartz

As stated in the previous chapter, clear quartz crystals are one of the most popular, easily accessible and versatile of crystals. As stated earlier it's also known as the master healer as it is most commonly used for its effective healing properties. However, clear quartz can also be used to deflect negative energy and attract positive energy (Skon, n.d.).

Clear Quartz (Alusruvi, 2014)

In addition to this, clear quartz is extremely versatile and therefore can be extremely malleable to the holder's intentions. Considering this factor, it's vitally important that we set specific and clear intentions when working with clear quartz.

In regards to using the stone, it can be worn as a jewelry piece or kept in our home or workspace to ward off negative energy. However, it's important that when we first charge the crystal, we hold it in our hands and set the intention for it to assist us in our daily lives by guiding and protecting us.

Black Tourmaline

Black tourmaline is extremely powerful of a crystal for protection, and creating a positive living and work space. It's mainly used to clear a space, ground it, and ward off negative energy.

This stone can be used by placing it by the front door or in corners of the home/workspace to clear any negative energy from the space and, furthermore, ground the space. If you are experiencing working in a toxic environment, you can also place black tourmaline on your desk to ward off any negative energy and give yourself a good extra layer of protective energy.

Black Obsidian

This crystal is mainly known for attracting positive energy, and carries a calm and positive energy with it. Carrying black obsidian around with you can leave you with a constantly nice reminder to always remain positive and perceive situations from the brighter side.

You can use black obsidian crystals for any occasion; however, if you are experiencing a tough day, you can keep the crystal nearer to you where you can easily access it. This is especially notable for days or situations where you know you will be easily triggered or know that you need an extra form of a pick-me-up. Black obsidian carries a fantastic calming energy with it, which can help the wearer to remain calm and positive, especially when faced with tough situations.

Black Jade

Black jade is best known to help those who want/need to avoid negative or toxic individuals. This is especially important for those of us who have to deal with psychic vampires, as this crystal can greatly help us in decision making, as well as offer a fantastic form of support and protection!

Black jade can help us to better tap into our intuition and even help us steer clear of negative people and situations. However, if you are already dealing with this negativity, black jade can still help one to tap into their intuition and guide them in how to best handle the situation. In addition to this, black jade can even help its wearer to identify where the negative energy is coming from, if we're having trouble trying to find the root cause of the negative energy.

We can aim to treat black jade as an energy guardian, protecting and guiding us as we maneuver through our daily lives. We don't *only* need to turn to black jade for when we need assistance with toxic or negative situations, we can keep black jade around as an all-round protector on a daily basis. Therefore, we can use this crystal by keeping it near us throughout the day. We can also aim to take the crystal along with us whenever we're entering new and unfamiliar territory, such as going on a vacation, meeting new people, or going to a job interview.

Pyrite

Pyrite is known to be an extremely gorgeous stone that shimmers in stunning gold hues. These gold layers serve as a protective shield from the harmful effects that technology has on our mind and body.

Pyrite (Pircher, 2015)

Pyrite is used by placing a small cube of the stone between yourself and your computer while you work. Pyrite can also serve as an energy booster, to help us remain mentally stimulated, energetically recharged, and enhance our levels of creativity, focus, and productivity. This belief stems from the different colors that are reflected from the stone, as well as its strong powers to protect the mind and body from the negative effects of using technology.

Protection Herbs

Brewing and drinking herbal tea is a perfect example of the powerful, healing benefits of herbs. We have used herbs for centuries within our cuisine, beverages, and for their healing purposes.

Considering this, there is no doubt that magick workers and spiritual healers should also make use of herbs, flowers, and plants in their daily practices. Whether it's used to assist us with spellwork and rituals (or any form of magick), medicinal purposes, or even used to simply help us calm ourselves, ground ourselves, or enhance our focus, herbs are another all-round powerful tool that magick workers regularly include in their practices (Moody Moons, 2019).

In addition to the above, herbs, plants, and flowers are also believed to possess specific energetic powers and properties, similar to crystals and amulets. For example, rosemary was a powerful herb to carry around during the Black Plague, as it was believed to help protect its wearer. Within this section, we will explore a few of the most powerful herbs, plants, and flowers that one can use within their daily magick work for protection. One of the biggest benefits of the herbs we are going to explore is that they are all easily accessible and affordable, while also being extremely powerful tools to incorporate into our magick work!

Rosemary

First on the list is rosemary: this plant has been commonly used in witchcraft for centuries and is popularly believed to ward off negative energy. The 'spikes' on rosemary are believed to symbolize protection for its wearer, and can be used as a defensive mechanism.

Rosemary can be planted by the entry area of your home as a way to ward off any negative energies, especially of those who enter or pass your home. Alternatively, one can simply sprinkle dried rosemary around any entry points of the home (including windows) to help protect the home from any negative energies.

Garlic

Aside from garlic being a fantastically powerful ingredient in our cooking, and a powerful healing tool for the sick, garlic *also* serves as a protection tool against any harmful, negative, and malicious energies. It is believed to be so powerful that it was worn around one's neck to protect one's self from vampires (as made famous in Bram Stoker's book *Dracula*).

When using garlic, place a clove on each of the four Elemental corners of your space (whether it's your home, office, place of worship) to seal off the space from any negative energies. This will help ensure that the place remains sacred and protected.

Cinnamon

Cinnamon is another popular ingredient that many cultures use in their cuisine and beverages. Like ginger (described below), cinnamon also offers numerous healing properties, as well as providing a powerful spicy kick to any meal or beverage. However, cinnamon has also been used for sacred practices for centuries.

Well-known for its 'woody' scent, cinnamon can be burned to cleanse the air of impurities. A popular practice with cinnamon includes burning a stick of cinnamon on a disc of charcoal to create a cloud of protection. This practice can be done at any given time, however it has been popularly practiced during rituals, spellwork, and Moon festivals/phases.

Cinnamon is also generally associated with those who have passed on, which is why you may often come across cinnamon being used as a protection herb during paranormal encounters or investigations, ghost hunts, exorcisms, rituals, or when attempting to make contact with the dead.

Basil

Basil is another common household herb that's also packed with various medicinal and magickal properties, notably its protective properties. Basil is also known to be used to aid with romantic scenarios, as it's commonly used in spells to protect the heart from heartbreak (in regards to a romantic scenario).

One can wear basil essential oil on their clothes or skin for extra emotional protection, especially when entering a new relationship.

Cloves

Cloves are famously known to be extremely powerful for protection against negative energetic attachments. Magick workers consider cloves to be an essential ingredient in their spellwork cabinet.

If you sense tension within a social interaction, you can make use of cloves to protect any evil eye (envy, negative talk) that's targeted towards you.

It's also important to note that we should not engage in negative social interactions or conversations either, as this can also come back around to you. Remember: radiating positive energy is a strong form of protection against encountering negative energy.

Ginger

Ginger is yet another powerful ingredient known for its medicinal properties; however, it is also extremely versatile with its magickal properties. Ginger is most commonly known to protect one against nightmares.

If you or someone you know (especially children) are experiencing constant nightmares, you can place a piece of ginger under the bed or pillow to ensure that they are safe and protected.

If someone is experiencing a hostile or eerie feeling within their own bedroom, especially at night, then burning ginger incense sticks can also help to clean the air and bring about calmness. This can also be done once a month during the dark Moon phase to ensure that the area is constantly protected and cleansed, just ensure that a window is left open so that the scent can dissipate.

Sage

Finally, sage is another popular and well-known herb to work with. It's extremely popular due to its all-round purposes as a protection herb, and has also been used for centuries to cleanse spaces.

White sage is most commonly used for smudge wands (to cleanse spaces), and garden sage is known to be an all-round, all-purpose protection herb. More specifically, however, garden sage is extremely beneficial in helping protect someone against making poor decisions or excuses for someone (essentially, protecting someone against their own poor judgement).

Garden sage can be used to help you ground yourself and clear your mind, so as to protect you from acting on emotion or poorer decisions that can ultimately lead to deep regrets in the future. If you are entering a space or situation where you know you need to make important decisions, then you can keep garden sage near you or incorporate it into a protection spell/ritual to ensure that you make decisions in your own best interest.

Protection Jars

As we have explored the above variety of ingredients (herbs, crystals, amulets) for magick work, we can take these powerful objects a step further and create protection jars that can enhance the magickal protective powers of the ingredients within the jar.

This section is where things really start to get exciting, as we can get really creative with the protection jars. We can even make the jars more specific to the situations for which we need protection or good energy.

Protection jars, also referred to as a 'witch bottle' or 'spell jar,' were extremely popular during the 16th and 17th centuries

(Schwarcz, 2019). During this time, people shared a powerful belief that evil spells can be trapped within a bottle (witch bottle) as a way of protecting themselves from the directed effects of the evil spell. This was especially practiced by those who believed that they were experiencing a direct attack on them (in the form of an evil spell) cast by another malicious and ill-intended witch or warlock.

Creating protection jars, at the time, was also believed to be so powerful that, if the jar was properly prepared, it possessed not only the power to absorb the negative spell/energies, but also the power to reflect the spell back onto the witch/warlock who cast the spell. In the process of reflecting that spell back onto the witch/warlock, it was believed that this would hopefully influence the evil witch/warlock to remove the spell because of how much of their own suffering and torment they were experiencing. Since then, the belief and practice has remained a powerful way for witches, warlocks, and spiritual healers to fight off negative energies and spells cast onto them or their loved ones. Additionally, protection jars also serve the same sentiment whereby they absorb all negative energy within a space in order to keep the space and possessor of the spell jar safe.

Protection jars are essentially made by combining herbs, crystals, written spells, magick water, and other ingredients of intention, and then placed into a jar. The jar can then be kept by a windowsill, near an entryway, or even buried in the garden (Kyteler, n.d.). In doing so, the protection jar can then work to protect your home, family, and yourself in the process.

Protection jars work in a sense whereby the jar creates a wall of powerful, protective magick that will protect anyone and anything behind the jar. Naturally, smaller jars containing smaller or fewer ingredients will be less powerful and will cover you from fewer energies, while larger jars with more ingredients will protect you from more energies and will inevitably be more powerful. However, if you can only get a hold of smaller jars, you can create numerous smaller protection jars and place them in various places in your space to protect the space.

Protection Jar (Creator09, 2021)

You will have control over what you would like to fill your protection jar with, and this can be specific to what type of protection you would like. For example, if you'd like protection at work, you can fill your jar with crystals to protect you from the harmful energies from technology (pyrite crystals), herbs to assist with protecting you against gossip, sigils with affirmations, and so forth.

If you want the jar to protect your home or someone else's home, you can place it near a windowsill to be charged by the Sun and Moon, or placed under a bed to protect one from nightmares. If you are giving a jar to someone as a gift, make sure to tell them what the purpose of the jar is and how they should best use it and where they might place it.

Another creative way of creating a spell jar is by using old jar candles and recycling them into spell jars! This spellwork is practiced and provided by *Tip of the Moon*, and is a fantastic way to combine and harness the energies of both candle magick with the magick of a spell jar (Comiskey, n.d.).

This process is extremely powerful and impactful because it requires first starting off with candle magick and using this energy towards the final spell for the spell jar. *Tip of the Moon* suggests laying the ingredients out in front of the jar before the final spell as a form of an offering prior to working with the ingredients for the final spell, and combining everything together.

For this ritual, you will need a jar candle that has about ¹/₂ an inch of wax left in it, with a wick that you can still burn for the ritual. By lighting the candle when combining the ingredients into the jar, the burning of the candle will symbolize sealing all of the ingredients together so that they harmoniously and powerfully work within the jar, and with a clear understanding of the intention you have placed on the spell jar.

The next few steps required for this spell jar are as follows: defining your intention for the spell jar, choosing your specific ingredients to put within the jar, charging the ingredients with intention, filling the jar with the ingredients, sealing and decorating the jar, meditating with the jar, and finally, finding a purposeful place for the jar.

In regards to defining your intention, this is the most important step for any spell or ritual. Once you are clear with your intention, you will then be able to choose the best ingredients for the spell jar and charge them with that powerful intention. Therefore, before starting the ritual, make sure to ask yourself the intent of this process and what specific goal needs to be achieved with this spell jar. You can also use journaling and meditating over this intention to gain more clarity on it.

Thereafter, choosing the right ingredients is the next important stage. This step is a combination of knowledge of the ingredients you as a magick worker work with, as well as trusting your intuition. A spell jar can be filled with a number of ingredients, however, it's power lies in how the magick worker works with, understands, charges, and combines the ingredients, so be as creative as you'd like and take your time. A few ingredient categories you can consider are: herbs, flowers, grains, coins, charms or amulets, egg shells, feathers, bones, crystals, stones, shells, intentions, sigils, affirmations, oils, herb infusions, honey, vinegar, photos (if those photos are specific to the person you are helping), among many other options. One of the most important things you will want to consider when choosing ingredients for your spell jar is the significance of the ingredients. All the ingredients that you add into your jar must possess some significance or meaning towards the intention of the spell jar.

Next, charge the items with intention and speak your magick into each item. In this step, you can include laying the ingredients out in front of the jar and holding each ingredient in your hand one at a time, charging it and then placing it into the jar. This process can include speaking of why you're placing the ingredient into the jar and what you want it to do for you. Charging the ingredients can be done through your energy, breath, and words, or be left out under the moonlight or sunlight.

Once all items are in the jar, seal the jar; this is usually done using wax, however you can use string or ribbon to close the jar off. You can also use a chant or mantra while sealing the jar, as this will also help you to bind the spell together into one powerful and cohesive spell jar. When the jar is properly sealed off, take a moment with the jar by holding it in your hands while meditating. This can be done as often as you like and for however long as you'd like.

Finally, find a significant place for the jar so that it can best use its powers for your intentions. Places such as an altar will work if you would like to continue working with it (by constantly meditating with it), burying it in the backyard to keep something close, or front yard to attract something. Wherever you place the jar must also include how you would like to work with the jar moving forward.

The Protection Spells

Having discussed objects, idols, items, and herbs that serve to protect and deflect any negative energy, while also drawing in positive energy, we can now move onto figuring out how we as magick workers can take this one step further and incorporate such items within our spellwork and magic.

In the next few chapters we will be exploring powerful protection spells that make use of the items we have explored up to now. These spells are specific, powerful spells to assist with specific issues. For example, in this chapter we will be exploring a few all-round protection spells, powerful deflective protection spells against psychic vampires and psychic attacks, as well as a few spells to recharge our energy levels (which assists with the notion of radiating), and a few protection spells to cast away negative energies that come with issues, such as gossip, envy, and jealousy.

THE STRONG PROTECTION SPELL

The strong protection spell, as the name suggests, is a spell created by Noah Tempestarii from The Witchcraft Way (*A Strong Protection Spell*, n.d.). This spell can be used as a way to protect yourself or others from negative energies that could be directed towards you.

The strong protection spell can also work similarly to an evil eye, which can protect you from the negative energies and intent of others, including ill judgement, envy, jealousy, and so forth. This spell will help you to create a protective shield, in a sense, to block negative energies out so that they cannot affect you. In essence, this spell is another form of deflection.

You will need:

- coarse sea salt (enough to draw a pentagram; the size is dependent on your preference)
- five tea lights
- one black taper candle
- one taper candle holder

The process includes:

1. Use the coarse sea salt to draw a pentagram. Be conscious of the intention behind each point of the pentagram, which represents the four cardinal Earth points and a fifth point representing the spirit. The connection between all points (through the pentagram) signifies the ultimate unity between all points. This powerful symbol shows the unified energy of the

universe, as these points of the pentagram cover all elements which are crucial for life.

2. Charge the tea lights with your intention for this spell; this can be done by holding each tea light individually and charging each with the main intention of the spell, and then slowly breathing that intention onto each candle. Once charged, place one tea light candle at each point of the pentagram's star.

3. Charge the black candle with intention (similar to the process with the tea lights). The black candle is going to symbolize you as the tool that is bringing about the protective magick over you; therefore, you will want to charge the candle with the intention of protecting you from negative people/energy. Once done, place the black candle in the center of the pentagram (with the taper candle holder).

4. Next, use your hands and intention to visualize, call upon, draw, and cast an energy dome infused by the salt and candles. Once this energetic foundation is set for the spell, you can go ahead and light the candles. The energetic dome will then expand itself around you and protect you and the area around you.

5. As the dome of protective energy surrounds you, chant:
   "Banish the harmful and all bad.
   Keep out the anger and the sad.
   Ancestors, Angels and Spirit Guides,
   Guard me through my daily strides.
   Against all ill thoughts, hex and curse,
   A protective shield shall disperse.
   As I do will it,
   So mote it be!" (*A Strong Protection Spell*, n.d.)

The Simple Protection Spell

This spell is primarily used for spiritual and physical protection, and was first initiated by Jenna from The White Witch Parlour (*A Simple Protection Spell*, n.d.). This protection spell serves as a fantastic all-round, general protection spell when you simply need that extra pick-me-up. It can even be performed every fortnight or prior to spellwork or rituals just to provide extra protection, or it could be used when you enter new or unfamiliar territory.

You will need:

- white sage
- star anise
- rosemary
- oil and a burner/cauldron (include a tea light if the oil burner requires it)
- black salt
- protection stones
- a black candle
- mortar and pestle

The process includes:

1. If you prefer to start off your spellwork/rituals by first casting a circle, you can do so now. You can also include cleansing the space by smudging the space with sage, or even ensuring that stones and crystals that cleanse the space are present during this ritual.

2. Next, cast a circle in your workspace using the black salt, and then place the protection stones at each quarter of the salt circle.

3. Place the oil burner in the circle, and light the tea light or turn on the oil warmer (whichever process your oil burner uses) to warm the oil.

4. Combine a few leaves of white sage and dried rosemary into the mortar and pestle, then grind until the mix is coarse and combined. As you grind the mixture, be consciously aware of the energies of the herbs as you smell them and work with them.

5. Once the mixture is coarse and combined, pour the mixture into the oil. As you pour and combine the mixture to the oil, attune your energies to the energies of the herbs and allow it to raise your energy. While this process happens, tap into the deeper intention of the protection spell and become consciously aware and clear of this intention, thus allowing your energy to become aware and strengthened by the energies of the herbs, and the intention of the spell.

6. Finally, add the star anise into the mix. Place the star anise in a manner that's meaningful to you. You can also place intention in the star anise and the manner in which you offer it, so that this can enhance the power and purpose of the spell.

7. Finish the ritual with an incantation:
   "I seek protection and sound my alarm
   My body, mind, and spirit now safe from harm
   My aura a shield to help me stay strong
   I now block negativity in all that is wrong."
   (*A Simple Protection Spell*, n.d.)

THE GOSSIP PROTECTION SPELL

The gossip protection spell is a spell you can perform when they feel you are caught in the middle of social gossip or drama. This spell can help protect you from the negative gossip and lies from others, and thus keep you free from any negative energies being targeted or directed towards you. You can also use this gossip protection spell if you are meeting a new group of people and want to avoid the negative energies that come with gossiping and judgemental attitudes.

You will need:

- one small bottle with a pour spout in the lid
- a little vinegar to fill into the small bottle

The process includes:

1. If you're experiencing negative gossip, threats, intrusion, or intimidation that affects you in your home life, then stand outside and face away from your house. If you're experiencing maliciousness and gossip from your workplace, then stand outside and face the direction of your work. If the negative energy is coming from a neighbor or a friend, then stand outside and face the direction of that neighbor or friend's house.

2. Using your dominant hand, point your index finger towards the source of the negative energy (or in the direction from which you think it is coming), or point straight ahead if you're unsure or where the negative energy is coming from, and say: "Desist,

stop spreading lies, insinuations, defamations. All must cease."

3. Turn around to face the opposite direction, and pour a trail of vinegar behind you as you walk towards your home. It's important to remember not to look back.

4. Pour the remainder of the vinegar under a cold running tap, repeating the spell until the bottle is empty and the vinegar has thoroughly been washed down the drain. Then throw the bottle away.

THE PROTECTION SPELL AGAINST A KNOWN ENEMY

This spell is also as the name suggests: it provides protection over a person who is encountering a traumatic, painful, unpleasant, or negative experience with another person. This spell does require needing to know who the other person (who is *causing* the pain) is.

Protection Spell Against an Enemy (Altmann, 2012)

For example, if you have to deal with someone who is causing you physical, emotional, mental, or even spiritual pain, and you can identify this person, then this spell will help you to deflect the negative energy back onto the person who was sending it.

You will need:

- dried tarragon/parsley
- one dark-colored glass bottle with a lid/cap
- milk that is beginning to curdle or sour

The process includes:

1. Pour a bit of dried tarragon/parsley into the bottle, then pour in the milk until the bottle is half full.
2. Close the bottle off with its lid and then start to shake the mixture. While doing this, state the person's name (who you want to deflect the negative energy back onto) eight times. Then repeat this spell eight times: "Bottle up the evil to me [or name the person who has been hurt and you are assisting] done. The pain is contained and all darkness is gone."
3. Place the bottle outside and leave it there overnight. In the morning, dispose of the bottle in a trash can or, if possible, near the perpetrator's home or workplace. When disposing of the bottle, repeat the following: "Bottled up and gone away. Returned to [name of the perpetrator] there to stay."

THE SUNLIGHT PROTECTION SPELL

The sunlight protection spell is mainly used to help spell-casters feel more at ease and grounded, and thus, more confident to tackle more spellwork. If you're ever feeling anxious, troubled, or in a low-vibrational space, this spell can be cast to help you gain a greater sense of calm.

Sunlight serves as a fantastic tool for spell-casters too, as it can serve as a powerful way to recharge our levels of energy to then allow us to tackle greater energies, spells, and rituals. The sunlight protection spell is quick and can even be included in our daily routine; it can even be done before/ after the standing sun salutation (if you include that practice in your daily routine).

Sunlight Protection Spell (Guler, 2012)

You don't need any items for this spell, which also makes this spell extremely accessible and resourceful. It can also be done at any point in the day (when the Sun is out).

The process includes:

1. Face towards the Sun so that the sunlight is hitting your skin. Close your eyes and focus on the light tingling and warming your skin, allowing the Sun's magickal properties to contact your face and body. Feel the heat energize your being.

2. With your eyes closed, repeat the following three times: "I harness the power of the Sun to protect myself from negative energy."

3. Thereafter, slowly inhale and exhale, allowing your body, mind and breath to fall into a regulated and calm rhythm. Bask in that peaceful, stable state.

4. Once you feel recharged and at a calmer state, you can gently open your eyes and then continue about your day.

THE ENERGY RECHARGING SPELL

This spell is similar to the Sun protection spell as it works towards recharging your energy levels; however, it's much more effective and intricate. It's primarily used as a spell on the occasion that one's energy levels are extremely low, or someone has encountered a negative person or scenario that was energetically draining, or someone has experienced a psychic attack.

If you or someone you are assisting is experiencing various low-vibrational side effects of a psychic attack and is in dire need of recharging their energies, then this spell is a perfectly powerful go-to spell.

You will need:

- one bowl of lukewarm water
- one bottle of essential oil of your choice (this can also include an essential oil that aligns with the intention of your spell; for example, lavender helps with tranquility and rose helps with love)

The process includes:

1. Add a few drops of the essential oil into the bowl of lukewarm water.
2. Place one of your palms facing upward (to the sky) and place the other downward, over the bowl of water.
3. Visualize the energy of the universe flowing down into your palm that's facing the sky, and then that energy flowing into you. You can envision this energy as a strong, luminous white light that's energetically recharging you as it makes its way through you. As you envision and feel this white light work through you, repeat the following: "I ask for the energy to stay active, healthy, and efficient. I ask to be replenished. I am a tower of strength and power."
4. Imagine that as the white light moves through you, it flows out of the other palm (facing the water) and flows into the water.

5. Once you feel that the bowl of water is sufficiently charged, wash your hands in the water, consciously noting that the water is charged with powerful, healing, and protective energy. Let the water work through your fingers and soak into your skin, noting that it should be a point to care for our physical body.

6. Take your time with this process and enjoy the moment, allowing the energized water to rejuvenate you. Repeat this process whenever you feel that you need to recharge your energy levels.

THE PHYSICAL PROTECTION SPELL

This spell is, as the name suggests, a powerful way to protect oneself from physical exhaustion and physical side effects that are triggered by low-energy or psychic attacks. Constantly battling with a psychic attack can exhaust us to the point where we experience various physical symptoms: from feeling fluish, to body aches, depression, headaches, and brain fog. Therefore, if you or someone you know are experiencing such side effects, this spell can be extremely useful.

You will need:

- 1 tsp of olive oil
- dried lavender
- ground cinnamon
- brown jasper
- one quartz crystal

- a small bag/pouch, just big enough to hold the crystal
- one small mixing bowl for the herbs and oil

The process includes:

1. Combine the herbs with the olive oil in the bowl, and mix well.
2. Hold the stones in your hand and declare: "I call on stamina to protect me from the exhaustion. I recharge my energy and defend my body, stamina, and endurance. I call on the crystal to always protect me."
3. Thereafter, dip your fingers into the oil and lather the oils onto the crystal.
4. Place the crystal into the small bag/pouch and carry the stone around with you for protection.

THE PROTECTION SPELL AGAINST PARASITES

Parasites (such as psychic vampires) can be an extreme headache to deal with. Parasites will stick on you and drain your energy and light, making it extremely exhausting to go about your daily life.

As we explored in Chapter 2, psychic vampires can come in various forms and leave us feeling constantly drained, exhausted, and even depressed. If you are dealing with a psychic vampire or parasite, you can make use of this protection spell to ensure that your energy levels are protected. This spell can also work hand-in-hand with various other energy recharging spells, such as the shield protection spell.

You will need:

- one clear quartz

The process includes:

1. Cleanse the quartz to ensure that you're charging the stone without any other residual energy left on it.
2. Next, ground yourself by focusing on your breath and tapping into the energy of the Earth, while also holding the stone in one or both hands.
3. As you draw energy from the Earth, imagine it flowing through you, down through your hands and straight into the crystal. As this energy transfer takes place, recite the following: "Crystal. With your endless power, support my light, support my energy, and cast this protection against those who wish to harm me."
4. Once you feel that the stone is sufficiently charged, gently bring yourself back to the present moment. You can then place the stone in your bag or pocket, or wear it as a jewelry piece so as to ensure that you carry the stone with you wherever you go.

Moon Spells and Banishings

As the previous chapter covered a good variety of protection spells and spells to recharge our own energy levels, this chapter is going to focus specifically on spells revolving around drawing energy from the Moon and its light.

All of the spells mentioned in this chapter can be done at any given time under the light of the Moon, however, it's naturally more powerful and beneficial when performed during the full Moon phase, as the full Moon's light is the strongest and most powerful.

Magick workers can draw on the energy of the Moon's light (similar to the Sun's light) to cast more powerful protection spells, banishing spells, or even simply draw from the Moon's energy to harness good energy, abundance, strength, healing, and prosperity. Whatever your intentions may be, it can be enhanced through the power of the Moon.

Full Moon (Ricard, 2016)

The Full Moon Spell

This full Moon spell is a fantastic all-round spell to recharge our energies and make use of the magick of the Moon (*Full Moon Spells & Rituals*, n.d.). This spell is also a fantastic option for those beginner magick workers who are fairly new to the magick of the Moon and how to tap into it. It's important to add that, as the name suggests, this spell requires being performed under the light of the full Moon.

This spell is fantastic in all aspects: it's easy, all-round beneficial, and doesn't require too many items. Therefore, if you would like to explore harnessing the powers and magick of the Moon, this spell is an amazing first step, or simply a great spell if you're in a rush but would still like to catch the magick of the Moon!

You will need:

- one clear jar
- water
- one silver coin
- one bell
- one candle, ideally a white one

The process includes:

1. First, start by identifying a wish or intention for this Moon spell and what you would like the Moon's magick to help you harness or achieve. This wish or intention can be anything you desire, whether it's protection, good luck, good health. Try to think of a clear, precise, and concise way to state your wish or intention, as you will be declaring this later in the ritual.

2. Fill the jar with water and light the candle. Place the jar and candle down, then find a spot to sit under the Moon and take a few moments to ground yourself. This can be done by closing your eyes and focusing on your breath.

3. When you feel calmer and more grounded, take the silver coin and place it into the jar of water.

4. Allow the water to resettle. Try to angle yourself so that if you look at the jar, you will see the reflection of the Moon sitting right on top of the coin. Sit quietly and gaze at the reflection of the Moon on the coin.

5. While gazing at the reflection, ring the bell three times and declare your wish or intention out loud.

6.   Once done, leave the coin in the jar (under the moon-
     light) until the next morning or until your wish/inten-
     tion comes true.

THE LUNAR PROTECTION SPELL

If you are looking for a good luck spell in regards to calling
upon abundance and protection, then this spell is a fantastic
go-to option (Huanaco, 2018)! Not only is the lunar protection
spell easy to do, it is also extremely resourceful and effective
for drawing in more good luck.

It's important to note that in order for the spellcaster to
reap the most benefits from the spell, it must be performed
under the light of the full Moon.

You will need:

- 1 tbsp of cloves
- one white candle
- water
- one shallow dish/side plate
- sage (incense or dried herbs)

The process includes:

1.   Light the candle and the sage (incense sticks, or the
     dried herbs in a fireproof container).
2.   Pour a bit of water into the shallow dish and then place
     the cloves into the water.

3. Ground yourself by closing your eyes, focusing on your breath, and clearing your mind. Once grounded, gently open your eyes and look at the Moon, or you can keep your eyes closed and visualize the Moon.

4. As you look at the Moon (or visualize it), imagine its protective white light and energy coming towards you and encompassing you. Continue to draw in that protective light until you're completely surrounded by the light, as if it were a strong shield of light around you.

5. As the light encompasses you, recite the following: "I incite the Protective Powers of the Moon, to wrap me in a powerful fire shield. To fill me with the Strength and Grade of the Earth. Winds bring me Wisdom, Water bring me Fortune. I let go of my fears so that I can keep in touch with the pulse of Life. Let this be done under the Moon and for the greater good of all. So be it, so it shall be!" (Huanaco, 2018).

6. Allow the candle to burn for as long as you please. As the candle burns, take a moment to meditate and release the magick and intentions of your spellwork into the cosmos.

7. When you are ready, extinguish the candle and pour the water and cloves into Nature, under the light of the Moon.

THE BANISHING CURSE

This spell is a powerful method to help deflect, ward away or banish any negative energies that are attempting to latch onto you. This spell can also help remove the evil eye, any ill-judgements or gossip placed on you from others, and even banish any curses placed on you by malicious or ill-intended people.

The banishing curse can also be performed if you or someone you are assisting is experiencing any side effects from a psychic attack.

This powerful banishing spell isn't only extremely effective, but also extremely quick, easy, and resourceful, as all you will need for this spell is one fresh egg.

The process includes:

1. Hold the egg to the center of your eyebrows, then move it down to the base of your throat, and then finally place the egg against your heart.
2. While holding the egg against your heart, recite the following: "Take from me this darkness sent, its powers I now give in you. The malice is gone, it is spent and through."
3. Thereafter, leave the egg at an intersection, or throw it against a tree so that the egg breaks.

THE BANISHING NEGATIVE ENERGY SPELL

Similar to the banishing curse, this spell also aims to banish any negative energy that's lingering in the air. Whether you're experiencing a psychic attack, being cursed, suffering from targeted negative energies, or simply need to banish negative energies that are lingering in your home or workspace, this banishing spell is a fantastic, all-round spell for such scenarios.

It should also be noted that this banishing spell doesn't only need to be used if one is aware of the presence of negative energies or negative influences. The banishing spell can still be used in any case to clear any negative energies, even if we aren't able to sense any. This spell can still serve to purify a space or place (*3 Wiccan Spells to Get Rid of Negative Energy*, 2017).

You will need:

- sage incense
- one silver candle
- sea salt
- water (in a small bowl or side dish)

The process includes:

1. Draw a circle with the salt, then light the candle and burn the sage. Place the bowl of water near your workspace.

2. This spell starts with the sage incense, which symbolizes the air element. Therefore, allow the sage smoke to fill the room while you sit in silence, calm your mind and ground yourself.

3. Once the sage has filled the space, place your hands over the incense and repeat the following: "With air I cleanse." and leave your hands hovering over the incense for a few moments before moving your hands over to the candle. Allow your hands to hover over the candle's flame as you proclaim: "With fire I cleanse." Hold your hands over the flame for a few moments before moving your hands over to the sea salt and state:

"With earth I cleanse." Finally, move your hands over to the water and then dip your hands in the water while stating, "With water I cleanse," all while keeping your hands in the water.

4. Remove your hands from the water and take a few moments to meditate, clearing your thoughts and grounding yourself in your wholeness.

5. Once you're ready, close the spell by proclaiming: "Any energy that serves me no longer, please leave now. Thank you for your presence. Now I am sending you home."

Protection Spells for
Your Loved Ones

In this chapter we are going to cover an extremely important topic: ensuring that our home, workspace, and loved ones are protected.

In earlier chapters we mentioned the importance of ensuring that we as magick workers are safe and protected before extending that energy outward. Now that we have covered a good variety of powerful spells to ensure that we are covered, we can move onto extending this energy unto our home, workspace, and loved ones.

We are all affected by energies, whether we're a magick worker or not. As magick workers, it's our responsibility to ensure the safety and protection of our space and loved ones while also ensuring that we aim to restore harmonious energetic balance within spaces and within people's lives. Therefore, in this chapter, we are going to learn how to extend our knowledge, powers, and protection unto others and their spaces.

THE HOME PROTECTION SPELL

This home protection spell is incredibly helpful if you feel that your home (or someone's home whom you're assisting) is being targeted by negative, ill-intended energy. This protection spell can also be performed even if you're unaware of the negative, targeted energy and simply want to ward away any lingering negative energy in your space!

However, if you are aware (or have a hunch) that your space may be bearing the brunt of malicious intent by a psychic attacker, then this spell can be extremely useful and powerful in order to cleanse the space, purify the energies, and bring about more harmonious balance in the space!

You will need:

- lemongrass
- sage
- ⅓ cup of rosemary
- ½ cup of sea salt
- lavender/clove
- a vacuum or broom
- sandalwood
- a container/jar (large enough to contain all of the ingredients above)

The process includes:

1. Combine the rosemary, lavender/clove, and sea salt into the container or jar, all of which contain cleansing and protective properties.

2. Place your hands over the jar/container, close your eyes, and envision a pure, white light below your hands (where the jar/container is). Once you are able to visualize the light, repeat the following: "With these herbs I cleanse this place so that everyone may enter without haste. With this salt this place shall start anew. Bad feelings out, away with the blues. As I will, so mote it be!"

3. Sprinkle a bit of the mixed herbs on the floors of each room within the place (especially near entryways and the four cardinal corners of the house).

4. Once done, take a seat and combine the lemongrass, sage, and incense. Burn the combination until it creates a strong cloud of smoke. Blow out the flame so that the mixed bunch of herbs is left burning smoke.

5. Take the incense and leave it in a room where there is usually a lot of physical activity, such as the living room, kitchen, or dining room.

6. Take the smoking sage and lemongrass and smudge your body, or over the body of the person you are helping. Smudging can also be done for other people who are residing in the house.

7. Once everyone has been smudged, you can then walk with the smudge around the house to cleanse the space, especially on the walls, doorways, and entrance of the home (this is where negative energies love to linger).

8. You can also smudge the perimeter of the house or yard if you'd like to, or if it feels necessary. Once done, you can put out the sage and lemongrass (or leave it

burning); however, leave the incense burning until it naturally burns out.

9. You can then vacuum/sweep up the herb mixture which you sprinkled on the floor, and then you can go about your day!

Home Protection Spell (Milovidova, 2020)

THE FAMILY PROTECTION SPELL AGAINST JEALOUSY

This Celtic circling protection ritual is specific to a family (or family members) receiving negative energies from others outside of the family who are jealous, envious, or ill-intended. This spell can be cast over a family to protect the family from the evil eye and remove any negative blocks or ill-intended targets towards them.

When one is prospering, thriving, or doing well, there is always the space open for others to judge, criticize, or become envious. Therefore, it's vitally important that we ensure that we cast protection over ourselves to ensure that the family is protected, and that they can prosper in peace. This spell can be done if we are visibly seeing and experiencing the effects of negative, jealous energy being directed towards us and our family, or this spell can simply be performed as a spell to cleanse and protect the energies of the family.

You will need:

- Photographs of each of the family members concerned. Place the photographs in the middle of a table (where the ritual will be performed) or in the middle of the room.
- Nine white flowers (preferably lilies) placed in a circle around the photos.
- An empty flower vase placed in the center of the table/room.

The process includes:

1. Start circling around the table or photos, and repeat the following: "Circle this home, Mother, Father, keep harm without, keep peace within. Circle this home, Mother, Father, keep all safe by day and night and bless them with the morning light." Alternatively, you can dedicate this to an angel you favor.

2. As you circle around the table and chant, take one flower at a time until you're holding all nine flowers.

3. Place the flowers one by one into the vase and state the following: "Blessings and protection on all" for each flower that you add into the vase.

4. Leave the flowers next to the photographs until they fade.

Family Protection Spell (Altmann, 2012)

THE BRACELET CHARM SPELL FOR YOUR LOVED ONES

This spell is cast onto a charm bracelet, which is a wonderful, powerful gift of protection to the receiver. This can be given to guard a child, anyone who is receiving ill-intentions or negative energies, or simply given to anyone as a gift for added protection.

You will need:

- one red coral or jet bracelet (for adults): one per individual you are empowering
- one jade or pink bracelet (for children): one per individual you are empowering
- one candle per bracelet; place each bracelet in front of its designated candle
- a bowl containing a mixture of salt and pepper

The process includes:

1. Hold one bracelet at a time and name the person you are intending on giving the bracelet to, then repeat the following: "May I/he/she be enclosed in this circle of love from all harm and ill intentions."
2. Light each candle as you work through each bracelet. As you light the designated candle for the bracelet, hold the bracelet to the candle's light and state: "May I/he/she be enclosed in this circle of light from all harm and ill intentions."

3. Sprinkle three circles of salt and pepper mixture around all candles and bracelets, in a counterclockwise manner. As you do so, state the following: "May I/he/she be enclosed in this circle of fierce protection from all harm and ill intentions."

4. Leave the contents as is until the candles have burned out.

5. Once the candles are burned out, dispose of the salt and pepper under a running faucet while stating the following: "Wash away all harm and ill intentions."

6. Once done, give the bracelets to the intended recipients.

JOB PROTECTION SPELL

This spell is powerful to perform whenever you sense any negative energy or tension surrounding you in regards to your work. This spell can also be cast if you feel that there is something blocking you from prospering in your career.

If you feel any negative or ill-intended energy surrounding this aspect of your life, this spell can be cast to clear that energy and bring about harmonious balance in this area of your life, or in your place of work.

You will need:

*   a mortar and pestle
*   one bottle with a cork/lid
*   sheepskin parchment paper.
*   1 tbsp of frankincense/myrrh

- 1 tbsp of iron filings
- 1 tbsp of sea salt
- 1 tbsp of oak moss/orris root powder
- one white candle
- black thread
- black ink (you can use a black ballpoint pen if this is easier to source)

The process includes:

1. Place the four ingredients of the tablespoons into the mortar and grind with the pestle, then set aside.
2. Cut a piece of sheepskin parchment (just enough to fit the inside bottom part of the bottle).
3. With the black ink, write the following: "I neutralize the power of my job to do me no harm. I ask that this be correct and for the good of all. So mote it be!"

Protection Spells Against Evil

It has become increasingly clear throughout this book that negative/evil energies are all around us. It's our job, as magick workers, to ensure that we restore harmonious energetic balance and banish evil spirits.

Due to the fact that magick workers are more aware of evil energies around the world, it then becomes our duty to ensure that we protect ourselves and our loved ones from such energies. While others may be suffering from psychic attacks, they may not be fully aware that it's due to negative energies being directed towards them. As we as magick workers are aware of these energies, we must take it upon ourselves to ensure that we keep our spaces cleared and cleansed, as well as ensure that we keep ourselves and loved ones protected. In doing so, this will clear their paths of negative blocks and start to welcome greater, positive energies in the forms of blessings, abundance, and opportunities.

THE BINDING SPELL

This spell can be used on unavoidable interactions with those who incite negative energies (such as through gossip, ill-intention, false lies, jealousy, envy). If you are encountering an unavoidable interaction or visitor who consistently causes problems or stirs drama and negativity, then this spell can be cast to "bind" their tongue with the symbolism of feathers and knots.

You will need:

- a dark-colored candle
- a long red cord
- nine feathers
- red string

The process includes:

1. Light the candle, then turn the cord and each feather counterclockwise around the candle while repeating the following incantation (for each feather): "Still your tongue, [name of offender], soften your words. Your unkindness shall no more be heard."
2. Use the red string to tie each feather onto the cord. As you make a knot for each feather, proclaim: "Bound are you from speaking nastily, barred from the wounding thoughtlessly."
3. Blow out the candle and then state: "Your power to hurt is ended, gone. Your power to harm is ended, done."

4. Take the cord with the feathers and hang it horizontally inside the front of your entrance door, or over an outside-facing window.

5. After 1 month, release the feathers outdoors and cut the knots while stating: "I release all negativity, transformed to positivity."

6. If the person still persists with their ill-intent, repeat this spell monthly with new string, cord, and feathers to protect your energy from theirs.

THE DEFLECTING SPELL

This spell can be cast to keep spiteful, ill-intent or malicious energies out of your way, and protect you from harm. This spell is extremely powerful to deflect any negative energies and judgements which are being directed toward you. Most importantly, if you know or have to encounter people who act like snakes and want to do everything in their power to spite or hurt you, this spell can be a powerful deflector of that energy and protect your own energy.

You will need:

- one red candle
- a wide-necked, screw-top dark glass bottle, or a dark glass jar with a lid
- garlic powder
- vinegar or cheap red wine
- dried lemongrass (optional)

The process includes:

1. Light the candle and work by it.
2. Take the bottle, open the lid, and hold it with both hands while stating the following: "You [think of the person's name] shall no longer spit your spite at me (or the person you are assisting). It is not right and ends this night."
3. Fill the bottle a quarter way with garlic powder while repeating the spell three times.
4. Add lemongrass into the bottle and repeat the spell six more times.
5. Fill the bottle to the top with vinegar or wine and then secure the lid. Shake the bottle nine times while repeating the following incantation nine times: "Hide your face in shame, you I do not name. You can no longer spit your spite at me (or the name of the person you are assisting). I am free."
6. Extinguish the candle and place the bottle at the back of a dark cupboard or shed (in darkness).

THE ANTI-BULLYING SPELL

This spell is extremely powerful and useful for any scenario revolving around bullying. If you (or someone you know) is experiencing bullying, whether it be at home, in a social setting, or at work, cast this spell to deflect any negative energy away from you (or the person you're protecting). This spell can help one to be protected against negative energies, judgement, envy, etc. while also protecting our own levels of energy.

This spell is also extremely easy and resourceful, as it doesn't require too many items for the spell to be cast. All you need is a shiny or reflective object, such as a hand mirror.

The process includes:

1. Before encountering the scenario whereby you experience bullying (for instance, before work, school, or a social encounter with your bully), sit down quietly and hold the reflective object in your hands.

2. Look into the reflective object and state the following four times: "I charge you powerfully, let none intimidate me. Reflect back approaching negativity that none with bad intent may reach me."

3. Place your reflective object between you and the route from which your bully may be approaching you. As the bully comes towards you, touch the reflective shield and say the following statement in your head: "Turn back, for me you can no longer crack. Take back what you inflict on me, for I strongly repel your negative energy."

4. If the bully turns into a tyrant or has an outburst, look into the bully's eyes and repeat the spell words as mentioned in step 3, in your head. Continuing silently chanting the spell and refusing to react until the bully leaves.

5. As soon as you get a moment, splash water onto the reflective part of the reflective object.

THE EVIL EYE PROTECTION SPELL

The evil eye has served as a powerful protective tool against negative energies, judgment, ill-intended people and envy for centuries. It's considered a sacred symbol and process to protect oneself against directed negative energies.

If you are experiencing symptoms of a psychic attack, such as strings of bad luck (in whatever form, such as health or financial issues), then this spell can be cast to ward off the evil eye. This spell can also be cast if you just need general protection against the evil eye, or if you are entering new and unfamiliar territory and require additional protection.

Evil Eye Protection (Marques, 2020)

You will need:

- one blue permanent marker
- one small pressure-sensitive label
- one double-sided reflective mirror, or an object that is shiny/reflective on both sides
- one orange candle
- a small dish of water with a few grains of salt, and a drop of olive oil in it

The process includes:

1. Use the blue permanent marker to draw an eye shape on the label, then stick the label onto the back of the mirror (or reflective object).
2. Light the candle and hold the mirror in a manner so that you can see the candle in it; then, flip the mirror around so that the candle illuminates the eye. While looking at the mirror, state the following: "[Name of perpetrator], your evil eye of envy, your glance of jealousy, reflected back shall be."
3. Sprinkle the water with salt and oil onto the unmarked side of the mirror, and repeat the chant (from step 2) as you do so.
4. Wipe the unmarked side of the mirror clean and then keep the mirror positioned in a way, so that when the perpetrator approaches you, the eye on the mirror is facing you and the shiny surface is facing outward.

THE EYE OF ENVY SPELL

If you are looking for another spell to protect you from the evil eye, this spell can also be cast; however, it's more effective when dealing with scenarios involving envy.

You will need:

- six white candles placed in a circle
- one rose or lavender incense stick
- your favorite piece of jewelry or a piece of jewelry with a blue stone in the center of it (symbolising an evil eye)
- a dish of sand or soil

The process includes:

1. Light each candle counterclockwise while repeating the following incantation for each candle: "Shield me from the eye of envy by night and day, that I may live harmoniously, free from jealousy from whatever source or cause."
2. Light the incense stick from the flame of each candle while repeating the spell words (from step 1) as you reach each candle.
3. Next, hold the piece of jewelry in your nondominant hand while repeatedly drawing an eye shape in the smoke of the incense stick. As you draw the eye in the smoke, repeat the words: "Turn away the eye from me, think not of me, speak not of me, act not against me, so is it decreed."

4. Extinguish the incense stick by placing the lit end downwards into the dish of sand/soil.

5. Thereafter, quickly blow out each candle in a counterclockwise manner.

6. The spell is complete. Whenever you feel under threat or your energy levels are being compromised by the evil eye, touch your jewelry piece for extra protection.

Full Moon Meditation

To end off this book, we have chosen to take this opportunity to highlight one of the most powerful scripts to ensure we recharge our energy levels efficiently and remain connected to the Earth, the cosmos, and their energies, thus heightening our intuitive levels, our energetic levels and our magickal powers.

Full Moon Meditation (Caliskan, 2017)

While meditation can help center and ground us, meditation under the full Moon will enhance our magickal powers, therefore making us more powerful magick workers. The meditation guide we are going to end with is a powerful way to help us ground ourselves and tap into the Earth's powerful, magickal energies.

Full Moon Meditation Preparation

This script can be performed at any given point in time, regardless of the phase of the Moon. However, reaping the most powerful benefits of this spell will be best received during a full Moon. A true full Moon phase usually lasts 5 days: 1 day where the Moon is at its fullest and 2 days prior and following the fullest Moon phase. Therefore, if you'd like to receive the energy from the Moon, try to perform this ritual during the main full Moon day.

Once you are ready to perform this session (especially if the Moon is full), find a quiet and serene spot where you can sit or lie down under the full Moon and look at the Moon. It's vitally important to try and find a spot where the moon's light can reach your skin.

Receiving the light from the Moon (especially during a full Moon, when the moonlight is at its fullest) is said to be extremely purifying. It's known to cleanse the skin and detoxify the Earth. Become consciously aware of the moonlight's healing and rejuvenating properties as you soak in the light.

Finally, ensure that the spot you choose to chant this spell is a comfortable and quiet spot, free of any distractions and isolated. You will want to be one with Nature, grounded, calm, and as focused as possible. This will help to ensure that you are receiving the full benefits of this session.

Once you are ready, grounded and comfortable, you can move onto working through the following Full Moon Meditation Scripture. This scripture is provided to us by Meditation Brain Waves (*Full Moon Meditation Script*, 2019). This meditation guide is a 12-minute meditation session, and follows the guide as provided in the section below.

Chakra Meditation (Caliskan, 2019)

Full Moon Meditation Script

Begin to take a long, slow and deep breath in, breathing out, and relaxing. You may close your eyes.

Know that whatever you feel during this session is okay for you, so just allow yourself to experience whatever comes or whatever doesn't.

When the moon is full, it is in perfect alignment with the sun, so that it is reflecting a filtered light towards you and the earth below. Many cultures across all times believe that the full moon each month cleanses all that it touches.

Allow yourself to become cleansed today, removing any old, stuck negative energies… becoming fresh and renewed for the new month ahead.

Begin to breathe deeply once more… the slower you inhale, the more fully you can breathe. The slower you exhale, the more relaxed you become.

Inhale...cleansing energy…

Exhale...relaxing…

Inhale… feel the full moon beaming above you…

Exhale… relax…

Inhale… Imagine the moon round and full…

Exhale...relax…

Inhale… see the moon shining so brightly that it is almost hard to look at…

Exhale…into deeper relaxation…

The rays of the moon are beginning to cleanse you…starting on the surface of your skin…

Feeling how impurities and toxins are slowly moving, becoming loose and flowing…

The moon is high above you, but it feels so close…

Your skin is being cleansed by the moonlight…

Dropping all thoughts of your personal problems now…

Feel these worries and concerns melting away under the moonlight…

Each troublesome thought that arises about your life or your day, give it away to the moonlight…

Feel the moon gladly taking your troubles away…

Use this moment of opportunity under the full moon to let go completely…

Your mind is easily clearing our old ways of thinking…

This is a magickal evening… enjoy this cleansing process…

Feel your body renewing in the full moon…. Each tiny cell is in the full process of regeneration…

You can feel the old cells being shed, opening space for new cells to flourish…

Now, allow yourself to release any and all obstacles that have stood in your way...

Now is the opportunity under the full moon to let go of any hindrances that have become trapped in your own nature...

Feel yourself finally breaking through anything that has held you back...

All barriers that you couldn't see over before are crumbling to the ground...

Imagine the moon shining so brightly above you...

Allow for it to open you up on all levels of your awareness...

Feeling any stagnant energy becoming unstuck...

Now, you are beginning to clearly see, a new vision is coming through... a vision that was once lost...

This newfound vision is greater than anything you have ever seen before...

What do you see in your pure vision?

Do you see yourself accomplishing great things?

Perhaps you are fully healthy and vibrant...

Making amazing advancements in your career...

Having meaningful connections with people who believe in you...

Let the magick of the moonlight fill you with new ideas towards a better life…

You deserve to let go of the old in order to usher in the new…

Now, you may open your eyes and gaze up at the moonlight… see the moon and its giving nature…

You have been blessed with this cleansing session… the full moon will return for you next month, ready to take away all that holds you back…

Breathe in deeply one last time, feeling like a new version of you… and open your eyes.

(*Full Moon Meditation Script*, 2019)

Conclusion

As we come to a close, we have to re-emphasize one key factor: how truly, beautifully, empowering being a witch, warlock, spiritual healer, and magick worker is!

We possess the power to be both sensitive and aware of the magickal energies around us, but also understand the power we possess to manipulate energies (and the direction of them) for the greater good. We are able to be physical conductors of positive influences within this world by protecting our loved ones and spaces, banishing negative energies, deflecting ill-intended energies back unto their perpetrators, restore energetic balance in spaces, cleanse spaces, and even serve as a positive influence to draw upon more positive energy.

As we stated previously, being a witch is extremely empowering; however, with great power always comes great responsibility! We at Vibe with Light want to reemphasize the importance of taking care of yourself (energetically and spiritually) and in the most sustainable manner before extending your power, protection, and energy to others. While we possess immense, beautiful powers, we want to still ensure that they are being managed in the most efficient and sustainable way, which is why we aimed to highlight chapters (such as the last chapter) on ensuring that you are recharging your own energy shield in order to work as powerfully as you're intended to.

Second, we would like to remind you that behind all magick lies intention: in order for your magick work to be as powerful as you'd like it to work, you need to ensure that your intentions are pure, concise, and clear. As positive influences in this world, we also need to use this as a guideline for all of our magick work, ensuring that our spells and rituals stem from positive and pure intentions.

In conclusion, a few brief benefits of protection spells can be summarized into the following points:

- We create safe, protected and secure environments, whereby we and our loved ones can live and work in peace.
- We can create positive atmospheres around us that can ensure that we live every day with joy and happiness.
- We can ensure protection spells are put in place to remove any obstacles from our path, thus, creating more peaceful and serene journeys in all aspects of our lives.
- Protection spells can improve all aspects of our lives, such as improving our relationships with others, as we're happier. It can also improve our health, as we are protected from psychic attacks and less stressed. Our work and finances can even be improved, as we can focus more on these aspects and be more productive without having to fight negative energies all day.
- We can be physically, emotionally, mentally, spiritually, and energetically protected with protection spells.
- Protection spells can remove negative energies *and* negative influences from our lives, which can help us live healthier lives.

- Protection spells can ensure happiness, positivity, gratuity, and prosperity are brought about, as the spaces are much lighter and more conducive for such factors to thrive.

It's truly inspiring and motivating to remind ourselves of our power and take this in stride. It also allows us to become much more powerful so as to fight for the greater good.

Therefore, with this in mind, we turn our attention back toward the point of *intention*. As magick workers, it's our job to ensure that we bring about a balance of both unintentional and intentional malicious harm. For example, there are malicious witches out there with ill-intentions and it is our duty to restore positive energy in those spaces. It is our duty and ability to transform spaces from negative energies to positive influences. We are responsible for the energy we create and draw upon within a space. Therefore, we naturally want to strive to create spaces conducive to positive influences, especially for ourselves and our loved ones.

Now, as magick workers, it's time to harness your energy and empower yourself to be a strong, forceful, positive influence in your world! It's time to take back your power and bring about peace, positivity, and harmony within your space for you and your loved ones' lives. Finally, if you are feeling overwhelmed by this responsibility, always know that we are conductors of the cosmos' energy. We have ample energy rechargers at our literal fingertips. If you are feeling overwhelmed, turn back to your energy recharging spells, make use of energy recharging crystals, and place more emphasis into your daily routine to ensure your energies are sufficiently recharged and you feel powerful enough to take on the world, because you can!

Have you enjoyed our eBook? Has it been beneficial, informative and inspiring to you? Well, we at Vibe with Light would *love* to hear your feedback! Feel free to leave us a review of how our eBook has helped you and what you found most beneficial! Thank you for coming along on this journey with us!

REFERENCES

3 Wiccan spells to get rid of negative energy. (2017, May 9). Spiritual Experience. https://spiritualexperience.eu/wiccan-spells-to-get-rid-of-negative-energy/

A simple protection spell. (2021, January 14). The Witchcraft Way. https://witchcraftway.com/spells/protection-spells/a-simple-protection-spell/

A strong protection spell. (2021, January 12). The Witchcraft Way. https://witchcraftway.com/spells/protection-spells/a-strong-protection-spell/

Alaska. (2020, June 12). *Blessing and protection spell—Meaning and benefits.* AstroTalk Blog. https://astrotalk.com/astrology-blog/blessing-and-protection-spell-meaning-and-benefits/

Caro, T. (2020a, July 19). *3 quick examples of a good luck Sigil.* Magickal Spot. https://magickalspot.com/good-luck-sigil/

Caro, T. (2020b, June 27). *Most powerful Wiccan protection amulets.* Magickal Spot. https://magickalspot.com/wiccan-protection-amulets/

Comiskey, B. (n.d.). *How to Make SPELL Jars & bottles with Candle Magick.* Tip of the Moon. Retrieved March 9, 2021, https://tipofthemoon.store/spells/spell-jars

Faragher, A. K. & Saint Thomas, S. (2018, April 9). *Why everyone's obsessed with healing crystals right now.* Allure. https://www.allure.com/story/healing-crystals-for-beginners

Full moon meditation script: 12-minute guided meditation. (2019, November 30) Self-Discovery & Transformation |. (https://meditationbrainwaves.com/full-moon-meditation-script/

Full moon spells & rituals: Everything you need to know. (n.d.). The Daily Struggle. Retrieved August 15, 2021, https://www.thedailystruggle.co.uk/full-moon-spells/

Garis, M. G. (2020, January 24). *A real Witch's 6 tips for using witchcraft to give your home an energy-clearing makeover.* Well+Good. https://www.wellandgood.com/how-to-cast-spell-home-energy/

Hart, A. (n.d.). *Do you know how to recognize a psychic attack?* The Traveling Witch. Retrieved August 11, 2021, https://thetravelingwitch.com/blog/do-you-know-how-to-recognize-a-psychic-attack

Hawthorn, A. (2021, February 3). *4 ways to protect yourself as a witch.* https://medium.com/witchology-magazine/4-ways-to-protect-yourself-as-a-witch-62f5a2d7500a

Herstik, G. (2017, June 26). *Ask a witch: How to bring witchcraft into your regular life.* Nylon. https://www.nylon.com/articles/ask-a-witch-bring-witchcraft-into-your-life

Herstik, G. (2018, March 12). *Ask a witch: All about candle magick.* Nylon. https://www.nylon.com/articles/ask-a-witch-all-about-candle-magick

Huanaco, F. (2018, November 9). *Lunar protection spell: Super easy full moon ritual.* Spells8. https://spells8.com/lunar-protection-spell/

King, D. (2011, February 9). Are you under psychic attack? *Psychology Today.* https://www.psychologytoday.com/za/blog/mining-the-headlines/201102/are-you-under-psychic-attack

Klug, L. (2020, February 9). *The grounding magic of tea ritual.* Ginger Tonic Botanicals. https://www.gingertonicbotanicals.com/blog/the-grounding-magic-of-tea-ritual/

Kyteler, E. (n.d.). *How to make a protection jar (ingredients & spell).* Eclectic Witchcraft. Retrieved February 8, 2021, https://eclecticwitchcraft.com/how-to-make-a-protection-jar-ingredients-spell/

Magic spells guide for beginners (9 safety tips to know). (2020, November 13). SF Weekly. https://www.sfweekly.com/sponsored/magic-spells-guide-for-beginners-9-safety-tips-to-know/

Marshall, R. (2016, January 4). *Destroying arguments and captivating thoughts: Spiritual warfare prayer as global praxis.* Taylor & Francis. https://www.tandfonline.com/doi/full/10.1080/20566093.2016.1085243

Moody Moons. (2019, June 8). *9 sacred Protection herbs & spices to know.* https://www.moodymoons.com/2019/06/08/9-sacred-protection-herbs-spices-to-know/

Parma, G. (2014, April 7). *Spell: An invisibility cloak.* Llewellyn Worldwide. https://www.llewellyn.com/spell.php?spell_id=5540

Protection spells—Powerful protection magick! The Witchcraft Way. (n.d.). Retrieved January 12, 2021, https://witchcraftway.com/spells/protection-spells/

Schwarcz, J. (2019, April 29). *Bottled superstition: Then and now.* Office for Science and Society. https://www.mcgill.ca/oss/article/bottled-superstition-then-and-now

Skon, J. (n.d.). *6 crystals to protect yourself from toxic people & negative energy.* mindbodygreen. Retrieved July 20, 2021, https://www.mindbodygreen.com/articles/crystals-for-protection

Stewart, T. (n.d.). *10 mini rituals for your daily spiritual practice.* The Witch of Lupine Hollow. Retrieved May 10, 2021, https://witchoflupinehollow.com/2018/10/18/10-mini-rituals-for-your-daily-spiritual-practice/

Stinson, A. (2019, October 28). *A witch taught me how to cast spells & they actually helped my problems.* Bustle. https://www.bustle.com/p/a-witch-taught-me-how-to-cast-spells-they-actually-helped-my-problems-18783696

Winkler, M. (2019, June 21). *How to prepare for a ritual.* Inked Goddess Creations. https://www.inkedgoddesscreations.com/blogs/the-inked-grimoire/how-to-prepare-for-a-ritual

All images sourced from Pixabay, https://pixabay.com

Made in United States
Orlando, FL
30 July 2024